How Much Is That in Real Money?

A Historical Price Index for Use as a Deflator of Money Values in the Economy of the United States

JOHN J. McCUSKER

Worcester
AMERICAN ANTIQUARIAN SOCIETY
1992

Reprinted from the
Proceedings of the American Antiquarian Society
Volume 101 · Part 2
October 1991

How Much Is That in Real Money?
A Historical Price Index for Use as
a Deflator of Money Values in
the Economy of the United States

JOHN J. McCUSKER

B UT how much is that in *real* money? It is a question that lurks
behind the mention of the price of anything in the past,
from the cost of George Washington's false teeth to the
worth of the gold doubloon that Herman Melville's Captain Ahab
nailed to his ship's mast as the reward to the first of his crew to
sight Moby Dick. Teachers of history mention prices or wages at
their peril, certain in the knowledge that someone will ask the
question and equally certain that they will have a hard time answer-
ing it. We who study economic history in departments of history
are expected to be able to pronounce immediately on the modern
equivalent of the Biblical shekel, of medieval Venetian money, and
of World War I reparations—for students and for colleagues both.
Economic historians in departments of economics presumably
have it easier because economists are supposed to be able to find
out such things for themselves, however difficult the exercise may
turn out to be. What follows is intended as a guide to all who would
like to compare the changing value of things over time in real
terms, at least with regard to the American economy.[1]

1. I wish to acknowledge with thanks the help of several people who have read and
commented on this paper.

<hr />

JOHN MCCUSKER, currently professor of history at the University of Maryland, College
Park, will become Halsell Distinguished professor of history and professor of economics
at Trinity University in fall 1992.

Writers on economic matters have long recognized the need to reduce prices to constant value terms if the comparisons they wish to draw are to make any sense. They have not been equally unanimous in their choice of what to employ as the standard against which to measure the value of other things. Indeed there have been considerable differences of opinion as to what makes the best basis for such comparisons. A continuing contender has been the worth of an individual's labor. Economic theorists as different as Adam Smith, Benjamin Franklin, and Karl Marx have argued for a labor theory of value. According to Smith:

> Labour . . . is the only universal, as well as the only accurate measure of value, or the only standard by which we can compare the values of different commodities at all times and at all places. We cannot estimate, it is allowed, the real value of different commodities from century to century by the quantities of silver which were given for them. We cannot estimate it year by year by the quantities of corn. By the quantities of labour we can, with the greatest accuracy, estimate it both from century to century and from year to year.[2]

2. Adam Smith, *An Inquiry into the Nature and Causes of the Wealth of Nations* (1776), edited by R[oy] H. Campbell, A[ndrew] S. Skinner, and W[illiam] B. Todd, 2 vols. (Oxford: Clarendon Press, 1976), I, 54. Cf. *ibid.*, I, 47, 51, 328–29. Despite what he stated in these passages, Smith elsewhere (*ibid.*, I, 67) rejected the notion, so essential to Marx, that labor was the exclusive determiner of prices in a capitalist economy. See Ronald L. Meek, *Smith, Marx, & After: Ten Essays in the Development of Economic Thought* (London: Chapman & Hall, 1977), pp. 7–8. For an introduction to this subject and a bibliography, see Donald F. Gordon, 'Value, Labor Theory of,' in *International Encyclopedia of the Social Sciences*, edited by David L. Sills, 17 vols. ([New York:] The Macmillan Company & The Free Press, [1968]), XVI, 279–83. See also Terence [W.] Hutchison, *Before Adam Smith: The Emergence of Political Economy, 1662–1776* (Oxford: Basil Blackwell, [1988]), pp. 364–65 *et passim*.

For Franklin, see his *A Modest Inquiry into the Nature and Necessity of a Paper-Currency* (Philadelphia, Pennsylvania: New Printing Office, 1729), pp. 18–23; and as reprinted with commentary in *The Papers of Benjamin Franklin*, edited by Leonard W. Labaree *et al.* (New Haven, Connecticut: Yale University Press, 1959 to date), I, 141–57. Note that, as William A. Wetzel pointed out in *Benjamin Franklin as an Economist*, Johns Hopkins University Studies in Historical and Political Science, 13th Ser., No. 9 (Baltimore, Maryland: Johns Hopkins Press, 1895), pp. 18–22, 30–32, Franklin borrowed heavily in this matter from both the ideas and the words of [William Petty], *A Treatise of Taxes & Contributions: Shewing the Nature and Measures of Crown-Lands* . . . (London: N[athaniel] Brooke, 1662).

For Marx, see his *Capital: A Critique of Political Economy*, edited by Friedrich Engels, translated and edited by Samuel Moore and Edward Aveling, revised by Ernest Untermann, 3 vols. (1867–94; Chicago: Charles H. Kerr and Co., 1906–09), I, 41–55 *et passim*. See also, Ronald L. Meek, *Studies in the Labour Theory of Value*, 2d ed. (London: Lawrence & Wishart, 1973).

Just as Adam Smith suggested, the two alternatives to his labor theory of value have been the value of precious metals, usually gold and silver, and the value of commodities. While the last of these, the value of commodities, has clearly won out as the accepted measure of changes in value over time, there are still those who agree with Smith that wage rates are the best deflator and there are others who prefer gold or silver. Commodity prices have the advantage of combining the value of the things that go into them, including the value of the work involved in producing them. The cost of commodities contains the value added by labor. The commodity price index has been and continues to be the preferred basis for comparing values over time.[3]

A commodity price index is a statistical tool designed to accomplish comparisons of real money values over time by filtering out from the data the impact of any differences in the value of money itself. The effect of using a commodity price index to answer the

The use of the value of labor as a long-term price deflator still has its proponents. See Stanley Lebergott, 'Wage Trends, 1800–1900,' in *Trends in the American Economy in the Nineteenth Century*, edited by William N. Parker, National Bureau of Economic Research, Studies in Income and Wealth, Vol. 24 (Princeton, New Jersey: Princeton University Press, 1960), pp. 449–99; Lebergott, *Manpower in Economic Growth: The American Record since 1800* (New York: McGraw-Hill Book Company, 1964); and the discussion in Alice Hanson Jones, *American Colonial Wealth: Documents and Methods*, 2d ed., 3 vols. (New York: Arno Press, 1978), III, 1728–29.

3. For some concerns about the use of precious metals for this purpose, see Earl J. Hamilton, 'Use and Misuse of Price History,'. in *The Tasks of Economic History: Papers Presented at the Fourth Annual Meeting of the Economic History Association — A Supplemental Issue of the Journal of Economic History*, [Supplement IV] (New York, 1944), p. 48; Hamilton, *War and Prices in Spain, 1651–1800*, Harvard Economic Studies, Vol. LXXXI (Cambridge, Massachusetts: Harvard University Press, 1947), p. 232.

Perhaps the chief obstacle to using precious metals or labor to construct long-term indexes is the lack of adequate data. Two recent books by Roy W. Jastram on the historical fluctuations in the value of precious metals testify to this difficulty: *The Golden Constant: The English and American Experience, 1560–1976* (New York: John Wiley & Sons, [1977]); and *Silver: The Restless Metal* (New York: John Wiley & Sons, [1981]). He encountered considerable problems finding data for the period prior to the beginning of the nineteenth century and relied instead on nominal mint values and other official government sources rather than market prices. Compare John J. McCusker, *Money and Exchange in Europe and America, 1600–1775: A Handbook* (Chapel Hill, North Carolina: University of North Carolina Press, and London: The Macmillan Press Ltd., 1978), pp. 13–17; and K. N. Chaudhuri, *The Trading World of Asia and the English East India Company, 1660–1760* (Cambridge: Cambridge University Press, 1978), pp. 162–63.

question asked above is analogous to what one does using foreign exchange rates to convert foreign currencies into one's own money in order to make more comprehensible the prices of goods and services in other places. Even the calculations involved, simple division or multiplication, are much the same in both cases. The numbers produced, if only because they permit us a clearer view of the reality behind the original figures, are often referred to as the 'real' values. More usually, in comparisons of prices or trade data, we talk of the original figures as having been expressed in 'current' dollars (or pounds or yen) and the indexed prices as being expressed in 'constant' dollars (or pounds or yen).[4]

A commodity price index is only one kind of index number. Index numbers, which effectively reduce data series to percentages, may be calculated for any serial data, not just for prices. An index number 'measures the magnitude of a variable relative to a specified value,' called the reference base.[5] We resort to the index in order to enhance our perception of changes in a series by expressing the data as a percentage of a reference base. The index

4. There are several wide-ranging introductions to the subject among which the first two are considered masterworks. See Wesley C. Mitchell, 'The Making and Using of Index Numbers,' in *Index Numbers of Wholesale Prices in the United States and Foreign Countries*, United States, Department of Labor, Bureau of Labor Statistics, Bulletin No. 284 (Washington, D.C.: United States Government Printing Office, 1921), pp. 7–114; and Irving Fisher, *The Making of Index Numbers: A Study of Their Varieties, Tests, and Reliability*, 3d ed., rev. (Boston, Massachusetts: Houghton Mifflin Co., 1927). See also Walter R. Crowe, *Index Numbers: Theory and Application* (London: Macdonald & Evans Ltd., 1965); Bruce D. Mudgett, *Index Numbers* (New York: John Wiley & Sons, 1951); Jacqueline Fourastié, *Les formules d'indices de prix: Calculs numériques et commentaires théoriques* (Paris: Librairie Armand Colin, 1966); R[onald] F. Fowler, *Some Problems of Index Number Construction*, Studies in Official Statistics, Research Series, No. 3 (London: Her Majesty's Stationery Office, 1970); and Ralph Turvey, *Consumer Price Indexes: An ILO Manual* (Geneva, Switzerland: International Labour Office, 1989). For a useful overview of the subject, see Erik Ruist, Ethel D. Hoover, and Philip J. McCarthy, 'Index Numbers,' *International Encyclopedia of the Social Sciences*, ed. Sills, VII, 154–69. These essays include valuable bibliographies.

At least one unfortunate historian confused 'real' with 'actual' (as opposed to nominal) and wrongly labelled a current value series of export figures as the 'real' values. He wishes here to recant his error. See John J. McCusker, 'The Current Value of English Exports, 1697 to 1800,' *William and Mary Quarterly*, 3d Ser., XXVIII (October 1971), 607–28.

On the appropriateness of the concept of 'real' prices or 'real' values for historical analyses, see Robert William Fogel, *Without Consent or Contract: The Rise and Fall of American Slavery* (New York: W. W. Norton & Company, 1989), p. 432, n. 7.

5. Ruist, 'Index Numbers: Theoretical Aspects,' *International Encyclopedia of the Social Sciences*, ed. Sills, VII, 154.

number is the systematic expression of the percentage increases or decreases that any number in the series represents when compared against the reference base number.

Index numbers are especially useful for two purposes. They permit comparisons to be drawn among several parallel series more easily than we could from the disparate data. This is especially true when all of the index numbers are expressed in terms of reference base numbers dated to the same period. Index numbers are also useful because they transform the data in ways that allow for additional statistical analysis. Consequently they have been widely employed by economists, economic historians, and other researchers who deal with long series of numbers.

Using commodity prices to construct index numbers of the value of things has an impressive pedigree. In the eighteenth century, at least three major European political economists employed commodity price indexes in their analyses: the Englishman Bishop William Fleetwood, the Frenchman Charles Dutot, and the Italian Count Giovanni Carli.[6] The Massachusetts General Court put theory into practice in the 1740s and again in the 1780s by legislat-

6. [William] Fleetwood, *Chronicon Preciosum: or, An Account of English Gold and Silver Money, the Price of Corn, and Other Commodities, . . . &c. in England, for Six Hundred Years Last Past*, [rev. ed.] (London: T[homas] Osborne, 1745); [Charles de Ferrare Dutot], *Réflexions politiques sur les finances et le commerce. Où l'on examine quelles ont été sur les revenus, les denrées, le change étranger, & conséquemment sur notre commerce, les influences des augmentations et les diminutions des valeurs numéraires des monnoyes*, 2 vols. (The Hague: V[aillant] and N[icolas] Prevost, 1738) ; and Gian Rinaldo Carli, *Delle Monete e dell'Instituzione delle Zecche d'Italia, dell'Antico, e Presente Sistema d'Esse e del loro intrinseco Valore, e Rapporto con la Presente Moneta dalla Decadenza dell'Imperio sino Secolo XVII*, 4 vols. in 3 (Mantua: [n. p.], 1754; Pisa: Giovan Paolo Giovannelli, e Compagni, 1757; and Lucca: Jacopo Giusti, 1760). For discussions of these works see Mitchell, 'Making and Using of Index Numbers,' in *Index Numbers of Wholesale Prices*, pp. 7–10; Fisher, *Making of Index Numbers*, pp. 458–60; and Crowe, *Index Numbers*, pp. 97–99 *et seq.* For a discussion of Fleetwood, who published his first edition in 1707, see G[eorge] N. Clark, 'The Occasion of Fleetwood's "Chronicon Preciosum",' *English Historical Review*, LI (October 1936), 686–90. Fleetwood's concerns were shared by his contemporaries. See, especially, the seventeenth-century debate over the property requirement for jurors as summarized in James C. Oldham, 'The Origins of the Special Jury,' *University of Chicago Law Review*, L (Winter 1983), 144–50. For a discussion of Carli, whose third volume, *Del Valore, e della Proporzione de' Mettali Monetati con i Generi in Italia prima delle Scoperte dell'Indie; Col Confronto della Proporzione de' Tempi Nostri*, is of particular interest, see Ch[arles] Coquelin and [Gilbert Urbain] Guillaumin, *Dictionnaire de l'économie politique*, 3d ed., 2 vols. (Paris: Guillaumin & Cie., 1864), I, 289–90.

ing early forms of indexing.[7] In the latter instance one impetus for legislative action was complaints about losses in the purchasing power of soldiers' pay caused by the depreciation in the worth of the state's currency. Similarly elsewhere over the last two centuries, episodes of sudden change in the purchasing power of money have whetted concerns about the commodity price index.[8]

The wider application of commodity price indexes has resulted in a sharpening of the theory of index numbers, a broadening in their application, more research into the history of price behavior, and the computation of more and better historical price indexes.[9]

7. Willard C. Fisher, 'The Tabular Standard in Massachusetts History,' *Quarterly Journal of Economics*, xxvii (May 1913), 417–51; and [Massachusetts (Colony), Laws, statutes, etc.], *The Acts and Resolves, Public and Private, of the Province of the Massachusetts Bay*, [ed. Abner Cheney Goodell *et al.*], 21 vols. (Boston, Massachusetts: Wright and Porter, 1869–1922), v, 1133–1137, 1277–1295. See the compiled 'mean rate of depreciation,' 1777–80, in *ibid.*, v, 1288. For the earlier example, see also *A Table Shewing the Value of Old Tenor Bills, in Lawful Money* ([Boston, Massachusetts: Samuel Kneeland and Timothy Green(?), 1750]); copy in the American Antiquarian Society, Worcester, Massachusetts. In 1780 the government of South Carolina addressed the same issue as the government of Massachusetts when it compiled and published a similar table. [South Carolina, Commissioners for Ascertaining the Progressive Depreciation of the Paper Currency], *An Accurate Table, Ascertaining the Progressive Depreciation of the Paper-Currency, in the Province of South-Carolina, during the Late Usurpation* . . . (Charleston, South Carolina: John Wells, 1781). Compare P. V. N. Vigneti, *Changes faits sur le cours des papiers-monnoies, depuis leur origine, 31 août 1789, jusqu'au 30 ventôse de l'an IV . . . auquel on a joint un tableau progressif de dépréciation vraie* . . . (Paris: Gueffier and the Author, 1797). See also Appendix C, below.

8. As one example, see the 'Aldrich Report' of 1893: [United States, Congress, Senate Committee on Finance], *Wholesale Prices, Wages, and Transportation: Report by Mr. [Nelson W.] Aldrich, from the Committee on Finance, March 3, 1893*, 52d Congress, 2d Session, Senate Report No. 1394 [Serial Set No. 3074 (4 parts)] (Washington, D.C.: United States Government Printing Office, 1893).

9. Arthur H. Cole and Ruth Crandall, 'The International Scientific Committee on Price History,' *Journal of Economic History*, xxiv (September 1964), 381–88, described much of the research done in the 1930s as an outgrowth of the monetary disruptions in the United States and Europe during the previous decade. See also *I Prezzi in Europa del XIII Secolo a Oggi*, edited by Ruggiero Romano ([Turin]: Giulio Einaudi, [1967]); and Gísli Gunnarsson, 'A Study in the Historiography of Prices,' *Economy and History*, xix (1976), 124–41. This research, only a part of which saw publication, provided the raw materials for most of the work that is the focus of this paper. For the United States, see especially the summary of the price history for the years before the Civil War compiled by Arthur Harrison Cole, *Wholesale Commodity Prices in the United States, 1700–1861*, 2 vols. (Cambridge, Massachusetts: Harvard University Press, 1938) . See also the works cited in n. 29, below. The most famous of the studies of European prices are William [Henry] Beveridge, *Prices and Wages in England from the Twelfth to the Nineteenth Century* (London: Longmans Green and Co., 1939); and N[icolaas] W. Posthumus, *Nederlandsche Prijsgeschiedenis*, 2 vols. (Leiden: E. J. Brill, 1943–64).

There are important collections of papers from all three of these studies, each containing

Both economists and historians have been active in these pursuits. Historians have employed the evolving theoretical constructs of the economist in their study of early economic behavior; economists have turned to the past in order to test and refine index number theory. Significant—not only as the occasion for this paper—is the progressively earlier application of all this research, for Great Britain back into the late medieval period, for the United States now to the beginning of the eighteenth century.

The attention given to commodity price indexes has also provoked research into the best ways to compile all index numbers.[10] This is especially true of index numbers that combine several elements, particularly general price indexes. The computation of a price index for a single commodity is a comparatively easy matter and involves the reduction of each value to a simple percentage of the reference base value, a 'price relative.' The computation of a general price index raises the issue of how to account for the differing degrees of importance among the various commodities

---

a great deal of additional material: Records of the International Scientific Committee on Price History, 1928–39, Manuscript and Archives Division, Baker Library, Graduate School of Business Administration, Harvard University, Boston, Massachusetts; William Beveridge Papers, Wages and Prices Collection, Manuscript Department, British Library of Political and Economic Science, London School of Economics and Political Science; and Collectie Commerciële Couranten, 15e–19e Eeuw, Economisch-Historische Bibliotheek, Amsterdam. For the Beveridge collection, see G. A. Falla, *A Catalogue of the Papers of William Henry Beveridge, 1st Baron Beveridge* ([London:] British Library of Political and Economic Science, 1981). For the materials Posthumus collected, see Peter Boorsma and Joost van Genabeek, *Commercial and Financial Serial Publications of the Netherlands Economic History Archives: Commodity Price Currents, Foreign Exchange Rate Currents, Stock Exchange Rate Currents and Auction Lists, 1580–1870*, Nederlandsch Economisch-Historisch Archief, Inventarisatie Bijzondere Collecties 4 (Amsterdam: Nederlandsch Economisch-Historisch Archief, 1991). See also the Frank Ashmore Pearson Papers, Albert R. Mann Library, Cornell University, Ithaca, New York; and the '(Industrial Research Department), Wholesale Prices' Collection, Wharton School of Finance and Commerce, University of Pennsylvania, Philadelphia. This last collection had yet to find a permanent home when I consulted it in May 1971; it was then in the care of the late Dorothy S. Brady of the Department of Economics, University of Pennsylvania.

10. This and subsequent paragraphs merely summarize the universally accepted (and, therefore, the non-controversial) points from the standard studies cited above. See n. 4 for the works by Mitchell, Fisher, and Crowe. Thus there are no detailed citations for what follows—unless some work states a point in a manner that seems particularly cogent. Furthermore, the discussion in Mitchell, 'Making and Using of Index Numbers,' in *Index Numbers of Wholesale Prices*, can be recommended as particularly rich for the economic historian and the explanations in Crowe, *Index Numbers*, as especially easy to understand.

the price relatives of which are to be merged into the single index number. For instance, if an index is composed of the prices of both diamonds and wheat, we have three choices: to assign each of them equal importance (or weight); to permit them to be 'self-weighted' proportionate simply to the differences in their money costs; or to impose some scheme for apportioning between them different weights based, perhaps, on some measure of their relative significance in an economy. The realization of the first and the last of these choices requires statistical processing of the price data before the index is computed. The second option, 'self-weighting,' while making the index easier to calculate, risks possible erroneous results, such as a price index that indicates a broad rise in prices when only the price of diamonds really rose.[11]

Compilers of modern price indexes, having the dual advantage of sufficient data and fast computers, are able to test very elaborate weighting schemes. By and large researchers have found that the best commodity price indexes are ones carefully weighted to reflect the relative importance of various commodities in an economy. Nevertheless indexes computed in all three ways tend to move roughly in tandem, changing direction at about the same time and to about the same degree. The key to the successful commodity price index rests in the choice of commodities. It is essential that one be sensitive to the 'utility value' of such commodities. As a consequence, self-weighted (or 'implicitly weighted') indexes that avoid eccentric commodities tend to be almost as good as weighted series.

Such results are reassuring to the compilers and users of historical series who rarely have enough data to construct weighted indexes and usually are forced by circumstances to adopt the weighting implicit in the differences in the magnitude of the prices themselves. Equally do we who work with historical series take comfort in the realization that commodity prices in any economy

11. Fisher, *Making of Index Numbers*, p. 333, cites two classic examples of 'freakishness' caused by eccentric commodities. On this whole subject see also *ibid.*, pp. 439–50.

are interdependent upon one another, that the price of flour, for instance, is a function of both the price of wheat and the costs of the labor and the machines to grind it, labor costs and machine costs being themselves influenced by the price of such things as bread. An index based on a few selected commodities can do almost as good a job of tracing the prevailing level of prices as can a weighted price index compiled from the prices of many different commodities. As one of the most important modern practitioners of the art, Earl J. Hamilton, has observed: 'Price historians have not infrequently discovered, to their dismay, at the end of a quarter century or more of assiduous labor that previously compiled index numbers based on the quotations of a very few articles — sometimes two or three — haphazardly thrown together from heterogeneous sources for widely scattered years have disclosed the trend of prices almost as accurately as their laboriously constructed indices from homogeneous series embracing monthly or quarterly quotations for dozens of commodities.'[12] The reason, according to Wesley C. Mitchell, perhaps the most important theoretician on the subject, is that 'the price changes of practically every commodity in the markets of the whole country are causally related to the changes in the prices of a few or of many, perhaps in the last resort of all, other commodities that are bought and sold.'[13]

12. Hamilton, 'Use and Misuse of Price History,' p. 50. Compare Hamilton, *War and Prices in Spain*, pp. 112–13.

13. Mitchell, 'Making and Using of Index Numbers,' in *Index Numbers of Wholesale Prices*, p. 39. Compare Fisher, *Making of Index Numbers*, pp. 331–40. Concerning Mitchell, see *Wesley Clair Mitchell: The Economic Scientist*, edited by Arthur F. Burns (New York: National Bureau of Economic Research, 1952).

It is necessary to reiterate the verdict of experts on this point because some writers seem willing to deny the usefulness of historical commodity price indexes based on a contention that a given index was compiled using too few commodities. See, e.g., Ralph Davis, *The Industrial Revolution and British Overseas Trade* (Leicester: Leicester University Press, 1979), p. 79; Leslie V. Brock, *The Currency of the American Colonies, 1700–1764: A Study in Colonial Finance and Imperial Relations* ([Ph.D. dissertation, University of Michigan, 1941]; New York: Arno Press, 1975), 'Preface'; Julian Gwyn, 'British Government Spending and the North American Colonies, 1740–1775,' *Journal of Imperial and Commonwealth History*, VIII (January 1980), 84, [n.] 12; and Peter H. Lindert, 'Probates, Prices, and Preindustrial Living Standards,' in *Inventaires après-décès et ventes de meubles: Rapports à une histoire de la vie économique et quotidienne (XIVe–XIXe siècles)*, edited by Micheline Baulant, Anton J. Schuurman, and Paul Servais, Actes du Séminaire Tenu dans le Cadre du 9ème Congrès International d'Histoire Économique de Berne (Louvain-la-Neuve, Belgium: Academia,

Another issue in the compilation of price indexes has to do with the mathematics of the actual computation. First, as suggested above, the question to be asked is: does one use the prices themselves directly, totaled and divided by the reference base number — the aggregate or 'market basket' method; or does one first compile a price relative series for each of the commodities and take the average of the several price relatives? Then, in considering the average to be calculated, one needs to decide whether to compute an arithmetic mean or some other measure of central tendency, perhaps a geometric mean.

Again the availability of a great deal of data for the modern period has allowed index number theorists to test out all the various options. The consensus seems to be, first, that an index based on an arithmetic mean is to be preferred because the resulting series can be manipulated statistically more easily than one based on the alternatives and, second, that the aggregate or market basket index is to be preferred because it can more easily be recomputed to a new reference base number thus facilitating comparisons. Nevertheless, as Irving Fisher wrote, 'from a practical standpoint, it is quite unnecessary to discuss the fanciful arguments for using "one formula for one purpose and another for another," in view of the great practical fact that all methods (if free of freakishness and bias) *agree!*'[14]

There are two types of general price indexes produced by these methods. The wholesale commodity price index and the retail

---

1988), p. 173. Thus the interdependence of prices in an economy needs to be emphasized, especially as it effects historical commodity price indexes.

Perhaps the most balanced and sensible comments in this matter are those of M[ichael] W. Flinn, 'Trends in Real Wages, 1750–1850,' *Economic History Review*, 2d Ser., XXVII (August 1974), 402: 'Frail and inadequate as the existing indexes are, objections to them can, however, be taken too far. Nobody seriously expects indexes for periods as far back in time as this to be exact within a per cent or two.'

14. Fisher, *Making of Index Numbers*, p. 231 (emphasis as in the original). Compare Hoover, 'Index Numbers: Practical Applications,' *International Encyclopedia of the Social Sciences*, ed. Sills, VII, 159. Note in this regard Robert E. Gallman's discussion of papers by Terry L. Anderson and Allan [L.] Kullikoff in 'Comment,' *Journal of Economic History*, XXXIX (March 1979), 311–12. Compare Earl J. Hamilton, 'Prices, Wages, and the Industrial Revolution,' in *Studies in Economics and Industrial Relations*, by Wesley C. Mitchell *et al.* (Philadelphia, Pennsylvania: University of Pennsylvania Press, 1941), p. 102, n. 6.

commodity price index are intended to describe two different but closely associated sets of price movements in an economy. The former has sometimes been called, perhaps more accurately, the producers' price index in that it is an index of the prices of primary market items. It is prone to more extreme fluctuations than the retail index not only in the short run but also sometimes even over longer periods. The retail price index is better described as the index of prices paid by consumers, the consumer price index. It is also known as the cost of living index, reflecting a primary purpose in calculating it. Its movements are less volatile than the wholesale price index. This is the index more properly used to deflate such things as wage rate series in order to test the changes in the real purchasing power of wage earners or to deflate estate valuations to measure changes in real levels of wealth. Those who construct historical price indexes, while ideally using retail prices, are sometimes faced with the necessity of turning to wholesale prices. Once again we can find reassurance in the knowledge that both types of prices are and were highly correlated. Where we have the opportunity of checking, the two indexes generally move in the same direction and change directions at the same time. The results of such compromises, born of necessity, are nonetheless satisfactory.[15]

'Satisfactory for what purpose?' the reader may ask. Economists, historians, and economic historians have turned price indexes to two purposes. First, and most important, price indexes have been used to trace and analyze the movement of prices across time. The price index itself allows us to describe the trend in, the cycles in, and even the seasonal variations in the average levels of prices, the last provided we have monthly or quarterly data. It is also possible to utilize a commodity price index to help make better sense out of the history of the price of a single commodity. Changes in the

15. For an especially germane discussion of this matter, see Paul A. David and Peter Solar, 'A Bicentenary Contribution to the History of the Cost of Living in America,' *Research in Economic History*, II (1977), 1–80, esp. pp. 15–17, 40–57. Compare Flinn, 'Trends in Real Wages,' p. 402: 'In the long run, and in many cases even in the short run, retail prices must move in sympathy with wholesale prices.'

price of each commodity have both common causes and more specific causes. Deflating a price series of an individual commodity using the commodity price index in effect filters out what was happening generally—those conditions that affected all commodities—and places in relief just what was particular to the price history of a specific commodity. In a similar fashion, we may use the commodity price index to deflate other economic series such as import and export data, wage rates, national product figures, and so forth, in order to understand better the real directions that they took, regardless of changes in the money in which they were measured.[16]

It should be obvious that there are dangers inherent in any simple cross-temporal or cross-cultural comparisons that fail to pay full regard to context. For instance, annual incomes of $25,000 in the United States today and an equivalent amount in, say, contemporary India mean considerably different things in terms of the earner's relative standard of living, social status, perhaps even political orientation.[17] Similar difficulties arise with comparisons over time and, indeed, are even more of a problem for being less obvious as well as for involving the technical problems of constructing indexes that accurately reflect real price changes. What

16. Commodity price indexes have also been used to 'index' such things as workers' salaries, payments under government social benefit programs, etc., in order to try to make them 'inflation proof.' See [United States, Department of Labor, Bureau of Labor Statistics], *BLS Handbook of Methods*, Bureau of Labor Statistics, Bulletin 2285 (Washington, D.C.: United States Government Printing Office, 1988), p. 157. Compare several of the papers in *Stabilization of the Domestic and International Economy*, edited by Karl Brunner and Allan H. Meltzer, Carnegie-Rochester Conference Series on Public Policy, Vol. 5 (Amsterdam: North-Holland Publishing Company, 1977).

17. 'That even the best index numbers designed to measure changes in purchasing power of money have numerous philosophical and mathematical defects every economist knows. *The purchasing power of money* is difficult to conceive and still more difficult to measure even within the limits of definite assumptions about the meaning of the term.' Hamilton, 'Use and Misuse of Price History,' p. 49 (emphasis as in the original). Compare Irving B. Kravis, 'Comparative Studies of National Incomes and Prices,' *Journal of Economic Literature*, XXII (March 1984), 1–39; W[alter] E. Diewert, 'Index Numbers,' in *The New Palgrave: A Dictionary of Economics*, edited by John Eatwell, Murray Milgate, and Peter Newman, 4 vols. (London: The Macmillan Press Ltd., 1987), II, 767–80; and the essays in Wolfgang Eichhorn, *Measurement in Economics: Theory and Application of Economic Indices* (Heidelberg: Physica-Verlag, 1988), pp. 49–164.

something is or was worth has much more about it than just a mathematical answer.[18]

The most important ramification of the greater attention to and application of commodity price indexes as a measure of changing price levels has been in the arena of public policy. We of the late twentieth century await the monthly release of the latest commodity price index numbers with some trepidation, having been taught to read in them one of the 'vital signs' of the economy. Nations with high rates of inflation are thought to have problems with their economies while the economies of nations with low rates of inflation are considered sounder. Governments with 'problem economies' are under considerable political pressure from a concerned populace to reduce inflation.[19] The commodity price index over the last two centuries has developed from a novel technique for validating price comparisons into a central element of public policy planning.

The second purpose to which commodity price indexes have been turned is one for which they were not designed and are not necessarily very well suited but a purpose which nevertheless has

18. There is consistent concern about these difficulties among the compilers of the indexes themselves. See, for instance, Franklin M. Fisher and Karl Shell, 'Taste and Quality Change in the Pure Theory of the True Cost-of-Living Index,' in *Value, Capital, and Growth: Papers in Honour of Sir John Hicks*, edited by J[ames] N. Wolfe (Edinburgh: Edinburgh University Press, 1967), pp. 97–139; and the essays and the items in the bibliography in *Price Indexes and Quality Change: Studies in New Methods of Measurement*, edited by Zvi Griliches (Cambridge, Massachusetts: Harvard University Press, 1971). It is these debates to which David and Solar, 'Cost of Living,' *Research in Economic History*, 11, 4–5, refer in their discussion of the dissatisfactions that neoclassical economists have with traditional, classical formulations of consumer price indexes. See also Melville J. Ulmer, *The Economic Theory of Cost of Living Index Numbers* (New York: Columbia University Press, 1949); and Robert A. Pollak, *The Theory of the Cost-of-Living Index* (New York: Oxford University Press, 1989).

Economic historians, who should not only be more sensitive than others to the complexities of such comparisons but also be better suited to deal with them, are in fact guilty of some of the most simplistic, even misleading use of price indexes. One economic historian who explored the issues carefully is Alice Hanson Jones, *American Colonial Wealth: Documents and Methods for the American Middle Colonies, 1774*, a separate number of *Economic Development and Cultural Change*, xviii (July 1970), 124–40. See also Lindert, 'Probates, Prices, and Preindustrial Living Standards,' pp. 175–76.

19. Consider as one example only the debate in Great Britain over the rate of inflation and the country's entry into the European Monetary System. See B. M. Craven and R. Gausden, 'How Best to Measure Inflation? The UK and Europe,' *The Royal Bank of Scotland Review*, No. 170 (June 1991), 26–37.

Fig. 1. The Consumer Price Index, United States, 1700–1840

NOTES AND SOURCES: Table D-1.

been sanctioned by long usage. We frequently see the fluctuations in a commodity price index discussed and displayed as if they described the fluctuations in the performance of an economy, as if the commodity price index ran parallel to the movement of the gross national product or were some sort of surrogate for it (compare Figure 1).[20] No one would deny that the two are interrelated if only because the prevailing price level and the performance of the economy as a whole reflect many of the same phenomena. Yet

20. It is a practice particularly popular with journalists and writers of textbooks. See, e.g., Gilbert C. Fite and Jim E. Reese, *An Economic History of the United States*, 3d ed. (Boston, Massachusetts: Houghton Mifflin Co., 1973 , pp. 160–61; Harold Underwood Faulkner, *American Economic History*, revised by Harry N. Scheiber and Harold G. Vatter, 9th ed. (New York: Harper & Row, [1976]), pp. 8–11; and Jonathan [R. T.] Hughes, *American Economic History*, 3d. ed. (Glenview, Illinois: Scott, Foresman and Co., 1990). Hughes states (p. 216): 'In an economy as free to respond to the signals of the market as was the antebellum economy [of the United States], general price movements indicate changes in the pace of economic life *in a rough way*' (emphasis as in the original). Compare Richard B. Morris, ed., *Encyclopedia of American History*, rev. ed. (New York: Harper & Row, 1965), pp. 536–41. W[alt] W. Rostow and Michael Kennedy, 'A Simple Model of the Kondratieff Cycle,' *Research in Economic History*, IV (1979), 1–36, offer an explanation as to why this was so. Compare Michael D. Bordo and Anna J. Schwartz, 'Money and Prices in the 19th Century: Was Thomas Tooke Right?' *Explorations in Economic History*, XVIII (April 1981), 97–127. See also Geoffrey H. Moore, 'A Truism: Recession Slows Inflation,' *New York Times*, Sunday, November 18, 1979, Business and Finance section.

neither would anyone who has lived in the United States over the past generation, or in any of the other countries of the capitalist world during eras of 'stagflation,' necessarily equate rising prices with a 'good' economy. If anything, as was mentioned just above, today, when we view the commodity price index as one of the vital signs of the economy, the correlation we draw may be just the reverse of the relationship implied in this use of the commodity price index by economic historians. Nevertheless, the argument can be made that stagflation is a new economic phenomenon and that, at least before the middle of the twentieth century, periods of rising prices generally corresponded well with periods of economic growth just as periods of falling prices were periods of economic decline. In other words, we can agree that cycles in price levels paralleled the business cycle.[21] Economic historians have indeed accepted this proposition and have relied on commodity price indexes to chart the course of the economy at least down to the time of the Great Depression and the New Deal.[22]

While it is certainly necessary that any who turn to a commodity price index be alert to all of these questions, at least in the very

21. 'Price levels . . . may be a fairly inexact index of swings of the business cycle, but for many centuries they have to suffice.' [Thomas C. Cochran], 'A Survey of Concepts and Viewpoints in the Social Sciences,' in *The Social Sciences in Historical Study: A Report of the Committee on Historiography*, [edited by Hugh G. J. Aitken], Social Science Research Council, Bulletin 64 (New York: Social Science Research Council, 1965), p. 85. Or, to quote Arthur F. Burns and Wesley C. Mitchell, *Measuring Business Cycles*, National Bureau of Economic Research, *Studies in Business Cycles*, Vol. 2 (New York: National Bureau of Economic Research, 1946), p. 75: 'Indexes of wholesale prices have served more faithfully as "barometers" of business cycles than many students now believe.' They date the divergence in the relationship between the two as something that began with the 1920s and 1930s. Compare Victor Zarnowitz and Geoffrey H. Moore, 'Major Changes in Cyclical Behavior,' in *The American Business Cycle: Continuity and Change*, edited by Robert J. Gordon, National Bureau of Economic Research, *Studies in Business Cycles*, Vol. 25 (Chicago: University of Chicago Press, 1986), pp. 554–55, and especially the papers by Robert E. Lucas, Jr., 'Understanding Business Cycles,' in *Stabilization of the Domestic and International Economy*, ed. Brunner and Meltzer, pp. 7–29, and by Finn E. Kydland and Edward C. Prescott, 'Business Cycles: Real Facts and a Monetary Myth,' *Federal Reserve Bank of Minneapolis Quarterly Review*, xiv (Spring 1990), 3–18. For a wider introduction to the subject, see Thomas E. Hall, *Business Cycles: The Nature and Causes of Economic Fluctuations* (New York: Praeger Publishers, 1990).

22. Including cycles in the early United States economy (see Appendix D). For evidence of the existence of the business cycle as a persistent feature of the economy over the centuries, see Raymond [A.] De Roover, *The Medici Bank: Its Organization, Management, Operations, and Decline* (New York: New York University Press, 1948), pp. 48–49.

broad terms outlined here, we need not concern ourselves with the details of their construction or application in order to employ them. Economic historians of the modern period are fortunate in that other scholars, better equipped than they to deal with these matters, have largely sorted out the issues and have already provided us with several good price indexes. This is particularly the case for the United States for the period from the late eighteenth century to the present (see Appendix A).

It is the articulation of price indexes for the earlier period in the history of the economy of the United States that one finds the primary contribution of this paper. In addition, the better to establish the relevance of this effort, the paper sums up and brings up to date various previously published series and discusses some minor matters rising from that work. These tasks are accomplished in the tables appended to this paper, most particularly in the summary Table A-2. Finally, there seems to be some merit in trying to explain more carefully how to compute price comparisons over time, especially as they apply to the seventeenth and eighteenth centuries.

An economist may wish to know how many 1987 dollars would be required to buy a house priced at $10,000 in 1953. To do so he or she has simply to turn to a table such as Table A-2 where, in Col. 6, one finds the commodity price index numbers for the two years in question and calculates the ratio between them $(1,359 \div 320 = 4.25)$. Using that ratio as a multiplier, one can establish that, if the costs of housing had increased over the years to the same extent as all commodity prices, a house priced at $10,000 in 1953 cost roughly $42,500 in 1987 dollars.[23] The computation is

23. Note that, in reversing the procedure, the ratio is employed as a divisor rather than a multiplier. Thus 42,500 1987 dollars, divided by 4.25, equals 10,000 1953 dollars. If one wanted to reduce several figures to a common denominator, a different procedure is required. It is possible, for instance, to state the values from both years in terms of 1860 dollars simply by dividing the two amounts by the index numbers for the respective years (1953 and 1987). It is necessary first to remember that the index number is in fact a percentage and, before using it as a divisor, to express it as one. Thus one divides 42,500 by 13.59 and 10,000 by 3.2. The quotient in both divisions is, of course, the same figure. The house was worth about $3,100 in 1860 dollars.

a simple one; the answer is mathematically sound; but the qualifying clause is all important. The result of such calculation is better considered as hypothetical rather than as definitive. In fact, because housing costs outran the average level of prices over the intervening three decades by some thirty-one percent, the kind of house that cost $10,000 in 1953 really cost about $55,000 in 1987.[24] The lesson is a valuable one not only because it exhibits one of the problems inherent in such comparisons but also because it shows the kinds of insights to be gained from their use. The commodity price index describes merely the central tendency in the movement of prices of all commodities.

Historians interested in the period before the American Revolutionary War do basically the same calculation, although with one additional step, and they must be even more cautious in their conclusions. Before the introduction of the dollar as the money of account of the new nation, the residents of each colony had their own distinct colonial currencies denominated in pounds, shillings, and pence (£1 = 20s. of 12d. each; £1 = 240d.). Because the commodity price indexes discussed herein are expressed in dollars, historians must first convert any eighteenth-century prices from pounds currency to dollars. This is most easily accomplished by reducing any sum in colonial currency to its equivalent in pounds sterling and then going from pounds sterling to dollars at the standard seventeenth- and eighteenth-century ratio of 4s.6d. sterling per dollar.[25] For example, in 1774, when the exchange rate was £135 Massachusetts currency per £100 sterling, £400 Massa-

24. [United States, President], *Economic Report of the President . . . 1990* (Washington, D.C.: United States Government Printing Office, 1990), p. 360. Compare the debate over the impact of housing costs on the British measure of inflation. See Craven and Gausden, 'How Best to Measure Inflation?' pp. 26–37.

25. It is better to do the calculation in this way, than to try to go from colonial pounds directly to dollars, because the ratio between dollars (pieces of eight) and sterling remained fairly stable over the seventeenth and eighteenth centuries while the ratio between dollars and each colonial currency varied considerably. The availability of currency-to-sterling exchange rates makes such calculations relatively easy. McCusker, *Money and Exchange in Europe and America*, collected and compiled rates of exchange. The traditional expression of sterling in pounds, shillings, and pence is here converted to a decimalized format (£1 = 100p) for ease of calculation. For example, 4s.6d. is rendered £0.225 or 22.5p. Compare McCusker, *Money and Exchange*, p. 323.

chusetts currency was the equivalent of £296 sterling.[26] At £0.225 sterling per dollar, or, inversely, 4.44 dollars per one pound sterling, £296 sterling was equal to $1,317. The two index numbers from Table A-2, Col. 6, for 1774 and 1991, are, respectively, 97 and 1,629; the ratio between them is 17 to 1; and £400 Massachusetts currency in 1774 works out to have been worth about $22,100 United States currency in 1991.

Using the explanation just given, it is possible for anyone to convert any sum in colonial currency to its approximate dollar amount today. Table A-3 shows the results of several additional examples and serves as a means of extending the discussion a bit further. For six colonies, for four periods of peace in the eighteenth century, each of them spanning a full economic cycle from peak to peak,[27] Table A-3 gives the equivalent in 1991 dollars of £100 currency. We can see that, for example, on the average over the years 1766–72, £100 Pennsylvania currency was roughly the value of $4,600 in 1991 terms. By extension, £10 Pennsylvania currency would be worth about $460, and £1 currency $46. If we recall that one pound equalled twenty shillings and one shilling equalled twelve pence, then we can determine that, on the eve of the American Revolutionary War, 1s. Pennsylvania currency was worth around $2.30 in 1991 dollars and 1d. about 19¢.

Comparisons of amounts from several different periods proceed in the same fashion. To determine the comparative worth of the legacies of two individuals whose estates were probated in, for example, Massachusetts in 1755 and 1855, one has simply to perform the same kinds of calculations outlined above. The first estate was inventoried at £1,750 Massachusetts currency; the second, $1,750. In 1755, £1,750 Massachusetts currency was the equivalent of £1,346.50 sterling or $5,983. From Table A-2, Col. 6, where the

---

26. McCusker, *Money and Exchange*, pp. 142, 317.

27. Following Bishop Fleetwood's dictum: ' . . . you must never take a very dear year, to your prejudice, nor a very cheap one, in your favour, nor indeed any single year, to be your rule, but you must take the price . . . for as many years as you can . . . .' Fleetwood, *Chronicon Preciosum*, pp. 135–36. The cycles are identified in Table D-1.

index numbers for 1755 and 1855 are 79 and 104, respectively, and the one for 1991 is 1,647, we can determine that $5,983 in 1755 was equivalent to about $123,400 in 1991 dollars and $1,750 in 1855, equivalent to $27,400. In real terms, the first estate was worth roughly four times the value of the second one.

The appearance of precision in all of these exercises, and, indeed, their inviting simplicity, should not obscure two important realities. We would be fortunate indeed if the data were good enough to allow us to be within ten percent of the true mathematical figure, meaning, for instance, that we can expect the actual worth of £100 Pennsylvania currency over 1766–72 to be something between $4,140 and $5,059 (1991).[28] While it is neater and computationally more convenient to use a mean rather than a range, we need to remember that a mean merely designates the central tendency within a range. Even more important, we should always remind ourselves that the mathematical answer to our question may not address all of the important issues. As with all other historical evidence, we need to evaluate it in context, we need to weight its implications in time and place, before drawing our conclusions. The price index as a deflator of money amounts over time is a tool, the 'real value' a means to an interpretative end, and never the answer in itself.

28. See in this regard Eric E. Lampard's suggestion as repeated by Sam Bass Warner, Jr., *Writing Local History: The Use of Social Statistics*, Technical Leaflet 7, rev. ed. (Nashville, Tennessee: American Association for State and Local History, 1970), p. 4. Compare the comment by M. W. Flinn quoted in n. 13, above.

APPENDIX A

CONSUMER PRICE INDEXES, UNITED STATES, 1700–1991

THE WORK OF MANY in compiling commodity price indexes for the United States was summarized, reviewed, and amplified in a 1976 article by two eminent economists. One can only be impressed by and thankful for Paul A. David's and Peter Solar's careful construction of an index of consumer prices in the United States over the previous two hundred years. The heart of their work was their Table 1 entitled 'Index of Consumer Prices, 1774–1974'; their series is referred to by them and hereinafter as the Brady-David-Solar index and is reproduced as Col. 3 in Table A-2.[29] While they acknowledged some earlier studies, they did

---

29. 'Cost of Living,' *Research in Economic History*, II, 1–80. They label their series the Brady-David-Solar index in recognition of their dependence on the estimates of Dorothy Brady (*ibid.*, p. 3).

Since that article appeared, others have produced complementary series of data. See, especially, Winifred B. Rothenberg, 'A Price Index for Rural Massachusetts, 1750–1855,' *Journal of Economic History*, XXXIX (December 1979), 975–1001. It is based on farm prices. In a comparison with price indexes at New York and Philadelphia 'the three series differ in the amplitude of their fluctuations, but in their periodicity with respect to the major economic events of that era they are markedly synchronous' (*ibid.*, p. 980). See also Donald R. Adams, Jr., 'Wage Rates in the Early National Period: Philadelphia, 1785–1830,' *Journal of Economic History*, XXVIII (September 1968), 404–26; and Adams, 'Prices and Wages in Maryland, 1750–1850,' *Journal of Economic History*, XLVI (September 1986), 625–45, based on his more extensive treatment of the same subject in 'One Hundred Years of Prices and Wages: Maryland, 1750–1850,' *Working Papers from the Regional Economic History Research Center*, V (No. 4, 1985), 90–129. Finally, see Donald R. Adams, Jr., 'Prices and Wages,' in *Encyclopaedia of American Economic History: Studies of the Principal Movements and Ideas*, edited by [Patrick] Glenn Porter, 3 vols. (New York: Charles Scribner's Sons, 1980), I, 229–46.

In addition to these indexes, four others have been compiled, three of them based on valuations in estate inventories. The two for Massachusetts in the seventeenth century are not satisfactory because they are based on extremely little data that are of questionable comparability. The one for Maryland (1658–1820) is not yet publicly available and, by its design, can and must be used only for deflating Maryland inventory values ('Maryland probate currency'). For the former, see William I. Davisson, 'Essex County Price Trends: Money and Markets in 17th Century Massachusetts,' *Essex Institute Historical Collections*, CIII (April 1967), 141–85; and Terry Lee Anderson, *The Economic Growth of Seventeenth Century New England: A Measurement of Regional Income* ([Ph.D. dissertation, University of Washington, 1972]; New York: Arno Press, 1975) and Anderson, 'Wealth Estimates for the New England Colonies, 1650–1709,' *Explorations in Economic History*, XII (April 1975), 151–76. Compare Anderson's comments on Davisson's efforts in Anderson, *Economic Growth of Seventeenth Century New England*, pp. 147–51. For the Maryland index, see references to it in the work of Lorena S. Walsh, 'Plantation Management in the Chesapeake, 1620–1820,'

not pay as much attention to others, notably the index generated by George Rogers Taylor and Ethel D. Hoover (hereinafter referred to as the Taylor-Hoover index) that reached back somewhat farther into the colonial era than did David and Solar themselves.[30] We can build on what they began.

David and Solar produced a consumer price index, as distinguished from an index of wholesale prices, in order to trace changes in the cost of living over time. Nonetheless they made the point, noted above, that there is considerable correspondence between the trends of wholesale prices and consumer prices both in their direction and in the timing of changes in direction.[31] Moreover they found these similarities to have

---

Journal of Economic History, XLIX (June 1989), 400, n. 8. The fourth index (Philadelphia, 1754–1800), compiled by Billy G. Smith, is of limited usefulness because his price data are institutional prices rather than market prices and because the index is weighted to emphasize the impact on the poor of the changes in the cost of a specified 'diet.' See Smith, '"The Best Poor Man's Country": Living Standards of the "Lower Sort" in Late Eighteenth-Century Philadelphia,' *Working Papers from the Regional Economic History Research Center*, II (No. 4, 1979), 1–70; and Smith, *The 'Lower Sort': Philadelphia's Laboring People, 1750–1800* (Ithaca, New York: Cornell University Press, [1990]).

30. [United States, Congress, Joint Economic Committee], *Study of Employment, Growth, and Price Levels: Hearings before the Joint Economic Committee, Congress of the United States ... April 7, 8, 9, and 10, 1959*, 86th Congress, 2d Session, 10 parts in 13 vols. (Washington, D.C.: United States Government Printing Office, 1959–60), Part Two: *Historical and Comparative Rates of Production, Productivity, and Prices*, pp. 379–410. The Taylor-Hoover index is reprinted in [United States, Department of Commerce, Bureau of the Census], *Historical Statistics of the United States, Colonial Times to 1970*, [3d ed.], 2 vols. (Washington, D.C.: United States Government Printing Office, 1975), II, 1196, Series Z 557. Cf. *ibid.*, I, 201, 204–06, Series E 52, 90, 111. See also the index compiled by Jones, *American Colonial Wealth*, III, 1719 (Table 3.5).

The Taylor-Hoover index for the colonial era was derived from the separate, earlier studies of prices at Philadelphia, Charleston, and New York originally published independently and later summarized in Cole, *Wholesale Commodity Prices in the United States*. We can find reassurance that these several different price histories are themselves reasonably satisfactory when we appreciate that, reduced to a sterling base, the prices in the various ports can be seen to have moved in parallel. For the original studies, see Anne Bezanson, Robert D. Gray, and Miriam Hussey, *Prices in Colonial Pennsylvania* (Philadelphia, Pennsylvania: University of Pennsylvania Press, 1935); Anne Bezanson, Blanch Daley, Marjorie C. Denison and Miriam Hussey, *Prices and Inflation during the American Revolution: Pennsylvania, 1770–1790* (Philadelphia, Pennsylvania: University of Pennsylvania Press, 1951); George Rogers Taylor, 'Wholesale Commodity Prices at Charleston, South Carolina, [1732–1861],' *Journal of Economic and Business History*, IV (February and August 1932), 356–77, 848–[76]; G[eorge] F. Warren, F[rank] A. Pearson, and Herman M. Stoker, *Wholesale Prices for 213 Years, 1720 to 1932*, Cornell University, Agricultural Experiment Station, Memoir 412 (Ithaca, New York: The University, 1932). For a slightly later period, compare Rothenberg, 'A Price Index for Rural Massachusetts, 1750–1855'; and Thomas Senior Berry, *Western Prices before 1861: A Study of the Cincinnati Market*, Harvard Economic Studies, Vol. LXXIV (Cambridge, Massachusetts: Harvard University Press, 1943).

31. David and Solar, 'Cost of Living,' *Research in Economic History*, II, 20–21.

been even greater in the earlier period, a fact that encouraged them, they argue, to project their index back into the colonial period relying almost exclusively on wholesale prices. 'We have therefore sought to infer the behavior of a consumer price index—which cannot really be constructed by direct means—from the observable movement of wholesale prices.'[32] It is a lesson the implications of which will be applied more broadly in the present discussion.

Taylor and Hoover compiled a wholesale commodity price index for 1720–1958 based on some of the same data that David and Solar later used; it is reproduced as Col. 4 in Table A-2. One can see immediately the sense of David and Solar's point quoted above: there is an increasing correspondence between the movement of the two indexes the further back in time that one looks. This suggests that it is not unreasonable to extend the Brady-David-Solar series even earlier into the eighteenth century. It can be done using the index compiled by Anne Bezanson that appears in Col. 2. The data in the Bezanson index, like those used by David and Solar for the later period, were compiled during the 1930s in a study of Philadelphia commodity prices undertaken by Anne Bezanson and her associates. On the basis of the Bezanson index, adjusted as David and Solar themselves adjusted their later data, the series in Col. 6 establishes a composite index that reaches all the way to 1720; the two are spliced at 1774.

As was just stated, two adjustments to the Bezanson index were necessary before the linkage was accomplished. In order to establish a consumer price index from data that were wholesale prices, David and Solar introduced a correction upwards; they determined the percentage of the correction through a 'markup adjustment model.'[33] On an average over the period 1774–94, this model resulted in an increment of 8.87%. The data that are the basis of the Bezanson index were also wholesale prices and they have been adjusted here by the same percentage.

The money of account in the United States during the period of the David and Solar index was the United States dollar, the basis of which was the Spanish peso de ocho reales, the piece of eight. During the American Revolutionary War, the paper currency depreciated in worth in comparison with the silver dollar (see Appendix C). David and Solar

32. *Ibid.*, p. 21. See also the discussion in Appendix B, below.
33. *Ibid.*, pp. 52–55.

also took this into account for the years 1774–84 by adjusting their index by 'an annual series of specie price relatives.'[34] It was necessary to do so in order that their prices would all be expressed in the same currency.

In the years before the American Revolutionary War, the money of account at Philadelphia was Pennsylvania pounds currency. An annual series of specie price relatives for the years 1720–74 was constructed on the basis of the exchange rate between Pennsylvania currency and pounds sterling. Pennsylvania currency was worth, at par, £166.67 Pennsylvania currency to £100.00 sterling. The dollar or piece of eight, was worth, at par, 4s.6d. sterling; £1 sterling was the equivalent, at par, of $4.44. The relationship of Pennsylvania pounds currency to specie varied directly as Pennsylvania currency varied against the pound sterling. Again the two series were spliced at the year 1774. While the figures in Col. 6 for the years 1720–73 are clearly less satisfactory as a consumer price index than are those for later years, there are reasons nevertheless for thinking it not wholly unacceptable.[35]

It is possible to extend the composite index back in time even further. Once again we can work from the same material that served as the basis of both the Bezanson index and the Brady-David-Solar index, the data collected by Anne Bezanson and her associates from Philadelphia prices. They amassed even more data than they published in their own books. Table A-1 is a compilation of some of those data, supplemented by information published elsewhere. In Table A-1 the data are organized into a commodity price index for the years 1700–20 precisely as Bezanson and Taylor-Hoover did for the later period but adjusted as above following the methods of David and Solar.[36]

There are one or two useful lessons from Table A-1. It exhibits, perhaps all too clearly, the very limited evidence upon which eighteenth-century commodity price indexes rest. While the other, later indexes avail themselves of more commodities, the number of commodities in any index, it has been argued above, are less significant than their nature. These are the wholesale market prices of five commodities that were

34. *Ibid.*, p. 49.
35. The overall correlation of all such indexes is the most significant of such reasons (see n. 29, above). Another reason is the crude but nevertheless comforting correlation between the United States commodity price index and that for Great Britain. See Appendix B.
36. Although none of those authors had a hand in compiling the index presented here in Table A-1, I have labelled it the Bezanson index to give credit to the source of most of the data.

central to the Pennsylvania economy at the time; they constitute an acceptable mix of imported and domestic commodities and of producers' and consumers' goods. Thus one can argue that they were reasonably representative in their own fluctuations of the movements of the other commodities in the same market. The index also exhibits the mode of calculating an aggregate or market basket index, unweighted (or, better, implicitly weighted), calculated using the arithmetic method. The index numbers appear again in Table A-2, Col. 1 and, spliced to the composite index in 1720 and recomputed to the new base period, in Col. 6.

Utilizing these same procedures, the Brady-David-Solar index in Col. 3, Table A-2, can be brought forward from 1974 through 1991, into 1992, and beyond. We accomplish this using the consumer price index compiled and published monthly and annually by the United States Bureau of Labor Statistics (see Col. 5, Table A-2). That, indeed, is the same index that David and Solar used for their index for the years 1914–74; here it is merely expanded a few more years. The reader can continue this same process by taking the monthly and annual index numbers as they are released by the Bureau of Labor Statistics and by splicing them into the series presented here.[37]

Linking these several series is critical to constructing the long-term

37. Used here is the CPI-U, the more broadly structured 'Consumer Price Index for all Urban Consumers (CPI-U),' on a reference base of 1982–84 = 100. The index number for any given month is announced by the Division of Consumer Prices and Price Indexes, Bureau of Labor Statistics (BLS), near the 20th of the next month. The index number for the year is announced by the same office near the middle of the following January. A recorded telephone message giving the latest figures is available at 1–202–523–1221. Technical questions are addressed at 1–202–272–5160. Since February 1978 the BLS has been compiling and releasing two index numbers, the result of a long-term project to revise the whole procedure of data collection and compilation. See [United States, Department of Labor, Bureau of Labor Statistics], *The Consumer Price Index: Concepts and Content over the Years*, Bureau of Labor Statistics, Report 517, rev. ed. (Washington, D.C.: United States Government Printing Office, 1978); *BLS Handbook of Methods*, pp. 154–215.

The BLS data series are republished in a number of places. Probably the easiest access to the most recent figures can be had in the tables distributed every month as the 'Summary of CPI News Release.' The BLS *Monthly Labor Review* contains both the data and analyses of both short-term and long-term price trends. The data are compiled and published every January or February in the presidential report on the state of the economy. In the *Economic Report ... 1991*, Table B-58 (p. 351) gives the BLS consumer price index annually for 1946–90 as well as monthly for 1989 and 1990. One can also consult the current [United States, Department of Commerce, Bureau of the Census], *Statistical Abstract of the United States* (Washington, D.C.: United States Government Printing Office). Various additional series and a most useful introduction to the whole subject are available as part of the *Historical Statistics of the United States*, 1, 183–214.

index necessary for extended comparisons. The process of splicing the two Bezanson indexes and the Bureau of Labor Statistics post-1974 index into the Brady-David-Solar index is necessary because each has a different reference base period. For all the indexes to be comparable, we must convert them to the same reference base.[38] The base year of the Brady-David-Solar series is 1860 = 100; the Taylor-Hoover index has the period 1850–59 = 100 as its base; the first Bezanson index uses 1700–02; the second Bezanson index, 1774; the Bureau of Labor Statistics series uses 1982–84 = 100.

The method of splicing is one that simply reduces the Bureau of Labor Statistics, the Bezanson, and the Taylor-Hoover series to a new reference base year, 1860 = 100. This linkage is realized in Table A-2, Col. 6. All that had to be done to accomplish the linkage is to change the annual number for Col. 6 by the same percentage that it changes in the other columns. For instance, according to the Bureau of Labor Statistics series (Col. 5), the increase in the consumer price index in 1978 over 1977 was 7.6% (161.2 ÷ 147.7 = 1.091). On base 1860 = 100, the composite commodity price index number for 1977 is 65.2 (Col. 6); an increase of 7.6% means that in 1978 the number with reference to this base is 780 (725 x 1.076 = 780). Should anyone wish to do so, a simple variation on this method will effect a change to a different reference base. One simply divides each annual number by the number for the year or years of the new reference base period.

The extension of the data in Table A-2, Col. 6, from 1700 to the present permits us to compare sums in real terms with those from any later time over almost the entire history of the United States.

38. For a discussion of the subject, with examples, see Hoover, 'Index Numbers: Practical Applications,' *International Encyclopedia of the Social Sciences*, ed. Sills, VII, 161.

COMMODITY PRICES AND COMMODITY PRICE INDEX,

PHILADELPHIA, 1700–1720

SHILLINGS PENNSYLVANIA CURRENCY

Year	Wheat (bus.)	Flour (cwt.)	Salt (bus.)	Rum (gal.)	Molasses (gal.)	Total	Total (Dollars)	Index
	1	2	3	4	5	6	7	8
1700	5.00	20.67	2.19	5.27	2.60	35.73	$102.45	95.6
1701	4.69	21.83	3.09	4.84	2.69	37.14	111.59	104.1
1702	4.39	19.56	3.98	5.90	2.61	36.44	107.45	100.3
1703	4.08	15.88	4.88	4.47	2.41	31.72	93.46	87.2
1704	3.94	14.79	4.17	3.52	2.30	28.72	85.10	79.4
1705	3.77	14.83	4.30	2.93	2.00	27.83	82.38	76.9
1706	4.09	16.39	3.95	3.00	2.21	29.64	87.48	81.6
1707	4.82	17.94	4.85	2.83	1.98	32.42	94.43	88.1
1708	5.31	19.50	3.57	3.88	2.39	34.65	100.03	93.3
1709	3.85	13.30	3.06	2.32	2.20	24.73	91.55	85.4
1710	3.42	11.86	3.14	2.26	2.23	22.91	79.45	74.1
1711	3.34	11.31	3.74	3.36	2.32	24.07	83.22	77.7
1712	3.41	11.94	5.45	4.23	2.34	27.37	94.35	88.0
1713	4.48	16.32	3.33	3.34	2.31	29.78	101.53	94.7
1714	4.03	17.01	3.76	3.48	1.78	30.06	100.83	94.1
1715	2.74	10.40	2.92	2.68	1.62	20.36	69.41	64.8
1716	2.52	7.59	2.41	3.00	1.53	17.05	56.75	53.0
1717	2.71	8.39	2.66	3.04	1.33	18.13	59.81	55.8
1718	2.33	11.31	2.60	2.94	1.62	20.80	69.92	65.2
1719	3.22	11.31	2.58	3.46	1.51	22.08	72.47	67.6
1720	3.08	9.25	2.31	2.68	1.34	18.66	59.77	55.8

NOTES AND SOURCES: The data in Cols. 1–3 were collected and compiled by Anne Bezanson and her associates and published in Arthur Harrison Cole, *Wholesale Commodity Prices in the United States, 1700–1861,* 2 vols. (Cambridge, Massachusetts: Harvard University Press, 1938), II, 1–6. See also, *ibid.,* I, 28. The data in Col. 4 and Col. 5 are from John J. McCusker, *Rum and the American Revolution: The Rum Trade and the Balance of Payments of the Thirteen Continental Colonies* ([Ph.D. dissertation, University of Pittsburgh, 1970] New York: Garland Publishing Inc., 1989), pp. 1096, 1104. Again, they come mostly from Bezanson via Cole, *ibid.,* II, 1–6. All figures are annual averages of the monthly data. Where there were fewer than twelve months available, means were first calculated for each of the quarters represented and then an annual average calculated from those means. The italicized figures are straight-line interpolations based on the neighboring data. All of these prices are wholesale prices and are subject to David and Solar's markup adjustment (see text). The figures in Col. 6 and Col. 7 are the totals in Pennsylvania shillings and dollars, respectively. The dollar figures were calculated by, first, reducing to sterling the totals in shillings Pennsylvania currency using the exchange rates in John J. McCusker, *Money and Exchange in Europe and America, 1600–1775: A Handbook* (Chapel Hill, North Carolina: University of North Carolina Press, and London: The Macmillan Press Ltd., 1978), pp. 183–84; and then by converting from sterling to dollars at the standard rate of 4s.6d. sterling per dollar (£1 = $4.44). The sharp change between 1708 and 1709 reflects the legal revaluation of Pennsylvania currency effective on May 1 in the latter year, a revaluation reflected also in the exchange rate, and one that is therefore filtered out in both the dollar figure and the index number. See McCusker, *Money and Exchange,* pp. 175–76. The index in Col. 8, reference base 1700–02 = 100, is an unweighted arithmetic index derived merely by dividing the other numbers in Col. 7 by the mean value in that same column for the years 1700–02.

CONSUMER PRICE INDEXES, UNITED STATES, 1700–1991

Year (Base =)	Bezanson (1700–02)	Bezanson (1774)	Brady-David-Solar (1860)	Taylor-Hoover (1859–60)	Bureau of Labor Statistics (1982–84)	Composite Consumer Price Index (1860)
	1	2	3	4	5	6
1700	95.6					130
1701	104.1					141
1702	100.3					136
1703	87.2					118
1704	79.4					108
1705	76.9					104
1706	81.6					111
1707	88.1					119
1708	93.3					126
1709	85.4					116
1710	74.1					100
1711	77.7					105
1712	88.0					119
1713	94.7					128
1714	94.1					128
1715	64.8					88
1716	53.0					72
1717	55.8					76
1718	65.2					88
1719	67.6					92
1720	55.8	83.5		58.6		76
1721		78.5		53.4		71
1722		82.7		55.5		75
1723		83.7		57.3		76
1724		88.3		60.4		80
1725		104.5		65.7		95
1726		101.1		68.7		92
1727		95.0		66.3		86
1728		88.9		63.1		81
1729		88.0		62.9		80

Year (Base =)	Bezanson (1700–02)	Bezanson (1774)	Brady-David-Solar (1860)	Taylor-Hoover (1859–60)	Bureau of Labor Statistics (1982–84)	Composite Consumer Price Index (1860)
	1	2	3	4	5	6
1730		88.3		66.6		80
1731		78.6		59.2		71
1732		73.6		58.0		67
1733		73.1		59.7		66
1734		73.6		67.0		67
1735		75.4		66.3		68
1736		71.4		62.6		65
1737		73.3		69.3		66
1738		78.2		69.4		71
1739		69.0		59.6		63
1740		72.6		59.6		66
1741		100.5		73.6		91
1742		89.7		69.7		81
1743		78.2		59.7		71
1744		72.9		57.1		66
1745		70.1		53.7		64
1746		71.9		55.0		65
1747		78.5		65.5		71
1748		90.6		74.3		82
1749		92.5		76.1		84
1750		92.7		73.9		84
1751		93.7		72.0		85
1752		95.6		75.6		87
1753		92.8		78.2		84
1754		89.5		71.4		81
1755		87.2		71.2		79
1756		85.3		69.5		77
1757		89.3		69.6		81
1758		95.6		73.9		87
1759		109.4		85.8		99

Year (Base =)	Bezanson (1700–02)	Bezanson (1774)	Brady-David-Solar (1860)	Taylor-Hoover (1859–60)	Bureau of Labor Statistics (1982–84)	Composite Consumer Price Index (1860)
	1	2	3	4	5	6
1760		106.5		81.5		96
1761		97.1		77.5		90
1762		104.7		83.4		95
1763		104.7		83.5		95
1764		96.7		77.2		88
1765		98.4		76.7		89
1766		107.6		81.7		98
1767		105.2		81.7		95
1768		99.7		80.7		90
1769		102.1		81.2		93
1770		109.9		80.0		100
1771		105.9		84.9		96
1772		120.6		98.2		109
1773		111.9		90.9		101
1774		107.1	97	84.3		97
1775			92	78.0		92
1776			105	108.0		105
1777			128	329.6		128
1778			166	598.1		166
1779			147	2,969.1		147
1780			165	10,544.1		165
1781			133	5,085.8		133
1782			146	139.6		146
1783			128	119.1		128
1784			123	112.7		123
1785			117	105.0		117
1786			114	105.1		114
1787			112	103.9		112
1788			107	97.4		107
1789			106	94.0		106

Year (Base =)	Bezanson (1700–02)	Bezanson (1774)	Brady-David-Solar (1860)	Taylor-Hoover (1859–60)	Bureau of Labor Statistics (1982–84)	Composite Consumer Price Index (1860)
	1	2	3	4	5	6
1790			110	99.9		110
1791			113	98.1		113
1792			115	101.3		115
1793			119	109.3		119
1794			132	121.7		132
1795			151	146.2		151
1796			159	158.0		159
1797			153	143.4		153
1798			148	139.2		148
1799			148	141.9		148
1800			151	140.6		151
1801			153	151.1		153
1802			129	128.8		129
1803			136	128.3		136
1804			142	136.0		142
1805			141	148.4		141
1806			147	139.8		147
1807			139	135.3		139
1808			151	122.0		151
1809			148	134.2		148
1810			148	136.9		148
1811			158	132.7		158
1812			160	136.9		160
1813			192	161.3		192
1814			211	184.4		211
1815			185	182.5		185
1816			169	176.9		169
1817			160	172.9		160
1818			153	168.6		153
1819			153	141.2		153

Year (Base =)	Bezanson (1700–02)	Bezanson (1774)	Brady-David-Solar (1860)	Taylor-Hoover (1859–60)	Bureau of Labor Statistics (1982–84)	Composite Consumer Price Index (1860)
	1	2	3	4	5	6
1820			141	116.5		141
1821			136	106.7		136
1822			141	112.7		141
1823			126	105.2		126
1824			116	102.4		116
1825			119	111.9		119
1826			119	99.5		119
1827			120	96.5		120
1828			114	95.6		114
1829			112	94.7		112
1830			111	90.6		111
1831			104	91.7		104
1832			103	95.0		103
1833			101	98.1		101
1834			103	94.6		103
1835			106	109.1		106
1836			112	122.2		112
1837			115	113.9		115
1838			112	110.1		112
1839			112	115.0		112
1840			104	94.9		104
1841			105	92.7		105
1842			98	80.8		98
1843			89	75.1		89
1844			90	78.0		90
1845			91	81.8		91
1846			92	82.5		92
1847			99	92.5		99
1848			95	78.4		95
1849			92	81.5		92

Year (Base =)	Bezanson (1700–02)	Bezanson (1774)	Brady-David-Solar (1860)	Taylor-Hoover (1859–60)	Bureau of Labor Statistics (1982–84)	Composite Consumer Price Index (1860)
	1	2	3	4	5	6
1850			94	90.6		94
1851			92	86.5		92
1852			93	87.6		93
1853			93	95.9		93
1854			101	102.7		101
1855			104	109.6		104
1856			102	109.5		102
1857			105	118.5		105
1858			99	98.2		99
1859			100	101.3		100
1860			100	99.6		100
1861			106	102.9		106
1862			121	119.5		121
1863			151	152.3		151
1864			189	220.9		189
1865			196	210.9		196
1866			191	197.4		191
1867			178	182.7		178
1868			171	177.3		171
1869			164	168.4		164
1870			157	149.1		157
1871			147	142.5		147
1872			147	151.6		147
1873			144	145.8		144
1874			137	138.0		137
1875			132	130.6		132
1876			129	120.3		129
1877			126	117.2		126
1878			120	100.0		120
1879			120	98.3		120

Year (Base=)	Bezanson (1700–02)	Bezanson (1774)	Brady-David-Solar (1860)	Taylor-Hoover (1859–60)	Bureau of Labor Statistics (1982–84)	Composite Consumer Price Index (1860)
	1	2	3	4	5	6
1880			123	109.6		123
1881			123	111.5		123
1882			123	116.3		123
1883			121	107.6		121
1884			118	99.9		118
1885			116	92.2		116
1886			113	88.8		113
1887			114	92.4		114
1888			114	94.2		114
1889			111	89.9		111
1890			109	90.8		109
1891			109	90.1		109
1892			109	84.3		109
1893			108	86.2		108
1894			103	77.4		103
1895			101	78.8		101
1896			101	75.1		101
1897			100	75.3		100
1898			100	78.3		100
1899			100	84.3		100
1900			101	90.6		101
1901			102	89.3		102
1902			103	95.1		103
1903			106	96.2		106
1904			107	96.4		107
1905			106	97.1		106
1906			108	99.8		108
1907			113	105.3		113
1908			111	101.6		111
1909			109	109.2		109

Year (Base =)	Bezanson (1700–02)	Bezanson (1774)	Brady-David-Solar (1860)	Taylor-Hoover (1859–60)	Bureau of Labor Statistics (1982–84)	Composite Consumer Price Index (1860)
	1	2	3	4	5	6
1910			114	113.7		114
1911			114	104.8		114
1912			117	111.6		117
1913			119	112.7		119
1914			120	110.0		120
1915			121	112.2		121
1916			130	138.1		130
1917			153	189.8		153
1918			180	212.0		180
1919			207	223.8		207
1920			240	249.3		240
1921			214	157.6		214
1922			200	156.2		200
1923			204	162.5		204
1924			204	158.4		204
1925			210	167.1		210
1926			211	161.5		211
1927			208	154.1		208
1928			205	156.2		205
1929			205	153.9		205
1930			200	139.5		200
1931			182	117.9		182
1932			163	104.6		163
1933			155	106.4		155
1934			160	121.0		160
1935			164	129.2		164
1936			166	130.5		166
1937			172	139.4		172
1938			169	126.9		169
1939			166	124.5		166

Year (Base =)	Bezanson (1700–02)	Bezanson (1774)	Brady-David-Solar (1860)	Taylor-Hoover (1859–60)	Bureau of Labor Statistics (1982–84)	Composite Consumer Price Index (1860)
	1	2	3	4	5	6
1940			168	126.9		168
1941			176	141.0		176
1942			195	159.6		195
1943			207	166.5		207
1944			210	167.9		210
1945			215	170.9		215
1946			233	195.6		233
1947			267	239.5		267
1948			288	259.4		288
1949			285	246.5		285
1950			288	256.2		288
1951			310	285.3		310
1952			317	277.3		317
1953			320	273.6		320
1954			321	274.1		321
1955			320	275.1		320
1956			325	284.0		325
1957			336	292.2		336
1958			346	296.2		346
1959			348			348
1960			354			354
1961			358			358
1962			362			362
1963			366			366
1964			371			371
1965			377			377
1966			388			388
1967			399			399
1968			416			416
1969			438			438

Year (Base =)	Bezanson (1700–02)	Bezanson (1774)	Brady-David-Solar (1860)	Taylor-Hoover (1859–60)	Bureau of Labor Statistics (1982–84)	Composite Consumer Price Index (1860)
	1	2	3	4	5	6
1970			464		38.8	464
1971			484		40.5	484
1972			500		41.8	500
1973			531		44.4	531
1974			589		49.3	590
1975					53.8	643
1976					56.9	680
1977					60.6	725
1978					65.2	780
1979					72.6	868
1980					82.4	985
1981					90.9	1,087
1982					96.5	1,154
1983					99.6	1,191
1984					103.9	1,243
1985					107.6	1,287
1986					109.6	1,311
1987					113.6	1,359
1988					118.3	1,415
1989					124.0	1,483
1990					130.7	1,563
1991					136.2	1,629
1992						
1993						

NOTES AND SOURCES: The dates in the table heading are the reference base periods (= 100). The figures in Col. 1 are from Table A-1, Col. 8. Col. 2 is from Anne Bezanson, Robert D. Gray, and Miriam Hussey, *Prices in Colonial Pennsylvania* (Philadelphia, Pennsylvania: University of Pennsylvania Press, 1935), p. 433. Col. 3 is from Paul A. David and Peter Solar, 'A Bicentenary Contribution to the History of the Cost of Living in America,' *Research in Economic History*, 11 (1977), Table 1, pp. 16–17. Col. 4 is from [United States, Congress, Joint Economic Committee], *Study of Employment, Growth, and Price Levels: Hearings before the Joint Economic Committee, Congress of the United States . . . April 7, 8, 9, and 10, 1959*, 86th Congress, 2d Session, 10 parts in 13 vols. (Washington, D.C.: United States Government Printing Office, 1959–60), Part Two: *Historical and Comparative Rates of Production, Productivity, and Prices*, pp. 394–97. For Col. 5 and Col. 6, see text and n. 37.

THE EQUIVALENT IN 1991 UNITED STATES DOLLARS OF £100
LOCAL CURRENCY FOR SIX OF THE CONTINENTAL COLONIES
AT FOUR PERIODS IN THE EIGHTEENTH CENTURY

COLONY	1713–19	1725–38	1766–72	1782–96
	1	2	3	4
Massachusetts				
Sterling Exchange Rate	173.26	361.84	131.46	
Equivalent in Dollars	256.51	122.83	338.09	333.33
1991 $ Equivalent	4,357.94	2,658.81	5,666.10	4,397.32
New York				
Sterling Exchange Rate	155.84	165.13	175.15	
Equivalent in Dollars	285.19	269.14	253.74	250.00
1991 $ Equivalent	4,845.13	5,825.89	4,252.49	3,298.02
Pennsylvania				
Sterling Exchange Rate	132.73	157.11	161.94	
Equivalent in Dollars	334.85	282.89	274.45	266.67
1991 $ Equivalent	5,688.82	6,123.44	4,599.41	3,517.93
Maryland				
Sterling Exchange Rate	128.25	133.62	160.81	
Equivalent in Dollars	346.56	332.61	276.38	266.67
1991 $ Equivalent	5,887.71	7,199.81	4,631.77	3,517.93
Virginia				
Sterling Exchange Rate	112.20	119.88	123.74	
Equivalent in Dollars	396.13	370.74	359.18	333.33
1991 $ Equivalent	6,729.82	8,025.09	6,019.48	4,397.32
South Carolina				
Sterling Exchange Rate	445.93	706.24	697.16	
Equivalent in Dollars	99.76	62.93	63.75	428.57
1991 $ Equivalent	1,693.25	1,362.22	1,070.18	5,653.73

NOTES AND SOURCES: Shown are the equivalents of £100 currency in both contemporary dollars and 1991 dollars. The periods are ones of peace over a full business cycle or two (peak to peak). The cycles are identified in Table D-1. The sterling exchange rates are the average annual rates over each period and are expressed as the amount of colonial currency equal to £100 sterling. The exchange rate data are from John J. McCusker, *Money and Exchange in Europe and America, 1600–1775: A Handbook* (Chapel Hill, North Carolina: University of North Carolina Press, and London: The Macmillan Press Ltd., 1978), pp. 315–17, as revised and augmented by additional research. For Massachusetts, Cols. 1 and 2 are in Old Tenor and Col. 3 in Lawful Money. For Maryland the figures are in Hard Currency. The dollar amounts in Col. 4 for 1782–96 are at the set ratios that applied after the American Revolutionary War as discussed in Appendix C and in n. 47. The 1991 dollar equivalents of the £100 currency figures are derived using the index numbers in Table A-2, Col. 6, as described above in the text.

APPENDIX B

CONSUMER PRICE INDEXES, GREAT BRITAIN,
1600–1991

THAT THE AMERICAN COLONISTS were subjects of Great Britain, that the economies of the colonies and the Mother Country were interconnected even interdependent, and that the economies of Great Britain and the United States continued to have a 'special relationship' down into the late twentieth century suggest a possible comparative element to any discussion of the commodity price index in the United States from the first days of the colonial period down to the present.

There are even more commodity price indexes for Great Britain than there are for the United States.[39] Again, however, others have done the job of sorting through them for us and selected those most useful for historical purposes.[40] If only because it was compiled on the same basis for so long a period and, as a result, satisfies the important criterion of consistency over such a long time, the index of English commodity prices used by most economic historians is the one generated by Ernest H. Phelps Brown and Sheila V. Hopkins. In compiling their index for the early period, Phelps Brown and Hopkins used the price data assembled during the 1930s by Lord Beveridge and his colleagues for the English price history project; for the last two centuries they relied more on the work of others. Their index spanned seven centuries from 1264 to 1954 on a reference base 1451–75 = 100; for the period 1600 to 1954, it is reproduced here in Table B-1, Col. 1.[41] For a comparison with another

39. For many of them, see Brian R. Mitchell, *British Historical Statistics* (Cambridge: Cambridge University Press, 1988) , pp. 714–36. Compare the discussion in Gerald Reitlinger, *The Economics of Taste*, 3 vols. (London: Barrie and Rockliff, 1961–70), I, xvi, II, xii, III, 9–17.

40. See, for instance, Flinn, 'Trends in Real Wages,' pp. 399–404, who concluded (p. 402) that 'the study of these indexes immediately brings out one feature which encourages one to take a slightly more positive attitude to them: that is their quite remarkable degree of agreement. Whatever criticisms might be made against this or that aspect of individual indexes, when juxtaposed it is their similarity of behaviour both in the short and long run that first impresses one.'

41. 'Seven Centuries of the Prices of Consumables Compared with Builders' Wage-rates,' *Economica*, New Ser., XXIII (November 1956), 296–314. This and related essays have been reprinted in Phelps Brown and Hopkins, *A Perspective of Wages and Prices* (London and New York: Methuen, 1981).

eighteenth-century commodity price index (reference base 1700–02), see the one by Elizabeth Boody Schumpeter and Elizabeth W. Gilboy as reproduced in Col. 2, Table B-1.[42]

It is possible to splice the Phelps Brown-Hopkins index into a retail price index compiled monthly by the Department of Employment and consequently to extend the British consumer price index down to the present. The original series on a reference base 1967 = 100 is reproduced here in Table B-1, Col. 3.[43] Table B-1, Col. 4, is a composite index combining the Phelps Brown-Hopkins series and the Department of Employment series. Linkage is accomplished at 1954. The reference base for Col. 4 is the same as that for Table A-2, Col. 6, 1860 = 100.

The Phelps Brown and Hopkins index continues to be used by economic historians of Great Britain although it has not gone without criticism. See the essay concerning it in E[dward] A. Wrigley and R. S. Schofield, *The Population History of England, 1641–1871: A Reconstruction* (Cambridge, Massachusetts: Harvard University Press, 1981), pp. 638–41. It does nothing to diminish the potential validity of any criticisms—though it may diminish their force—to indicate both that Phelps Brown and Hopkins recognized most of such problems themselves and also that many of the criticisms of their index emanate from a dissatisfaction with the results it generates for a particular piece of research. See, for instance, the comments by D[avid] [J.] Loschky, 'Seven Centuries of Real Income per Wage Earner Reconsidered,' *Economica*, New Ser., XLVII (November 1980), 459–65; or Donald [M.] Woodward, 'Wage Rates and Living Standards in Pre-Industrial England,' *Past & Present: A Journal of Historical Studies*, XCI (May 1981), 28–46. Compare H[arold] F. Lydall and E[rnest] H. Phelps Brown, 'Seven Centuries of Real Income per Wage-Earner Reconsidered: A Note,' *Economica*, New Ser., XLIX (May 1982), 201–05; and [Ernest] Henry Phelps Brown, 'Gregory King's Notebook and the Phelps Brown-Hopkins Price Index,' *Economic History Review*, 2d Ser., XLIII (February 1990), 99–103.

42. Elizabeth Boody Schumpeter, 'English Prices and Public Finance, 1660–1822,' *Review of Economic Statistics*, XX (1938), 21–37, and Elizabeth W. Gilboy, 'The Cost of Living and Real Wages in Eighteenth Century England,' *Review of Economic Statistics*, XVIII (1936), 134–43. Averaged here are the authors' two wholesale commodity price indexes for producers' goods and consumers' goods. Compare Phyllis Deane and W[illiam] A. Cole, *British Economic Growth, 1688–1959: Trends and Structure*, 2d ed. (Cambridge: Cambridge University Press, 1969), p. 14, and Figure 7; and McCusker, 'The Current Value of English Exports, 1697 to 1800,' pp. 617–19. The original Schumpeter-Gilboy indexes are reprinted in Mitchell, *British Historical Statistics*, pp. 719–20.

43. 'Prices are normally collected on the Tuesday nearest the 15th of the month and the result is available during the third week of the month following. It is issued to the press and later published in the *Ministry of Labour Gazette* [now the *Employment Gazette*].' Crowe, *Index Numbers*, p. 155. The monthly figures (now on a reference base January 1987 = 100) are also distributed in a mimeographed form by the Central Statistical Office and are published in its *Monthly Digest of Statistics* (since 1946). Recent quarterly figures and annual figures for the past fifteen years are published in [Great Britain, Central Statistical Office], *Annual Abstract of Statistics* (London: Her Majesty's Stationery Office, 1853 to date). The annual series is reproduced (through 1980) in Mitchell, *British Historical Statistics*, pp. 739–41. See in addition, the monthly, quarterly, and annual figures in the International Monetary Fund's *International Financial Statistics* (monthly).

An intriguing question for economic historians of early America is just how closely do the index numbers in Table B-1, Col. 4, correlate with those in Table A-2, Col. 6. The answer is: quite well indeed. For the period 1700 to 1790 the two moved in parallel tracks. They changed direction at roughly the same times and to roughly the same degree. Such parallels continued to operate through the nineteenth and into the twentieth centuries. Indeed, given the close connections between the two economies and the workings of such mechanisms as commercial and financial arbitrage, these parallels are to be expected, especially during the Old Empire.[44]

The parallels between the colonial and the British price indexes suggest three things. First, each index gains in credibility. The data for both commodity price indexes and, thus, the index numbers themselves are sound and can be relied upon as reasonably accurate in their depiction of the movement of commodity prices in each place. Second, our appreciation of the reality of the close connections among the economies along the Atlantic rim is buttressed. The British and the British colonial economies were clearly interrelated. The colonists were integrally tied to the Atlantic economy of which Great Britain, by the middle of the eighteenth century, was the leader.[45] Finally, the parallels of the eighteenth century and later suggest that the fluctuations expressed by the British commodity price index in the seventeenth century probably described colonial price movements fairly well during that century also, a period for which we do not yet have published adequate colonial commodity price indexes. One implication of all of these suggestions is explored more fully in Appendix D.

44. See below, Appendix D, and the works cited in n. 52.
45. Compare John J. McCusker and Russell R. Menard, *The Economy of British America, 1607–1789* (Chapel Hill, North Carolina: University of North Carolina Press, 1985), pp. 62–64, Table 3.4.

TABLE B-I

CONSUMER PRICE INDEXES, GREAT BRITAIN, 1600–1991

Year (Base =)	Phelps Brown and Hopkins (1450–1475)	Schumpeter-Gilboy (1700–1702)	Department of Employment (1967)	Composite Commodity Price Index (1860)
	1	2	3	4
1600	459			34.9
1601	536			40.8
1602	471			35.8
1603	448			34.1
1604	404			30.8
1605	448			34.1
1606	468			35.6
1607	449			34.2
1608	507			38.6
1609	559			42.5
1610	503			38.3
1611	463			35.2
1612	524			39.9
1613	549			41.8
1614	567			43.2
1615	561			42.7
1616	562			42.8
1617	537			40.9
1618	524			39.9
1619	494			37.6
1620	485			36.9
1621	461			35.1
1622	523			39.8
1623	588			44.7
1624	543			41.3
1625	534			40.6
1626	552			42.0
1627	496			37.7
1628	466			35.5
1629	510			38.8

Year (Base =)	Phelps Brown and Hopkins (1450–1475)	Schumpeter-Gilboy (1700–1702)	Department of Employment (1967)	Composite Commodity Price Index (1860)
	1	2	3	4
1630	595			45.3
1631	682			51.9
1632	580			44.1
1633	565			43.0
1634	611			46.5
1635	597			45.4
1636	593			45.1
1637	621			47.3
1638	707			53.8
1639	607			46.2
1640	546			41.6
1641	586			44.6
1642	557			42.4
1643	553			42.1
1644	531			40.4
1645	574			43.7
1646	569			43.3
1647	667			50.8
1648	770			58.6
1649	821			62.5
1650	839			63.8
1651	704			53.6
1652	648			49.3
1653	579			44.1
1654	543			41.3
1655	531			40.4
1656	559			42.5
1657	612			46.6
1658	646			49.2
1659	700			53.3

Year (Base =)	Phelps Brown and Hopkins (1450–1475)	Schumpeter- Gilboy (1700–1702)	Department of Employment (1967)	Composite Commodity Price Index (1860)
	1	2	3	4
1660	684			52.0
1661	648	115.1		49.3
1662	769	122.4		58.5
1663	675	116.8		51.4
1664	657	112.3		50.0
1665	616	115.7		46.9
1666	664	117.4		50.5
1667	577	116.8		43.9
1668	602	111.2		45.8
1669	572	103.3		43.5
1670	577	103.9		43.9
1671	595	106.1		45.3
1672	557	101.1		43.9
1673	585	103.1		44.5
1674	650	104.5		49.5
1675	691	106.7		52.6
1676	652	105.0		49.6
1677	592	98.8		45.0
1678	633	98.3		48.2
1679	614	101.6		46.7
1680	568	98.3		43.2
1681	567	94.9		43.2
1682	600	95.5		45.7
1683	587	96.6		44.7
1684	570	96.6		43.4
1685	651	93.2		49.5
1686	559	90.4		42.5
1687	580	85.4		44.1
1688	551	84.8		41.9
1689	535	88.2		40.7

Year (Base =)	Phelps Brown and Hopkins (1450–1475)	Schumpeter-Gilboy (1700–1702)	Department of Employment (1967)	Composite Commodity Price Index (1860)
	1	2	3	4
1690	513	96.0		39.0
1691	493	101.1		37.5
1692	542	94.9		41.2
1693	652	98.3		49.6
1694	693	102.8		52.7
1695	645	105.0		49.1
1696	697	113.3		53.0
1697	693	112.3		52.7
1698	767	111.3		58.4
1699	773	113.8		58.8
1700	671	104.1		51.1
1701	586	97.2		44.6
1702	582	98.7		44.3
1703	551	96.3		41.9
1704	587	97.2		44.7
1705	548	92.9		41.7
1706	583	96.8		44.4
1707	531	89.0		40.4
1708	571	91.9		43.5
1709	697	100.6		53.0
1710	798	110.9		60.7
1711	889	118.6		67.7
1712	638	96.8		48.6
1713	594	93.8		45.2
1714	635	94.3		48.3
1715	646	92.4		49.2
1716	645	91.4		49.1
1717	602	90.0		45.8
1718	575	89.5		43.8
1719	609	91.9		46.3

Year (Base =)	Phelps Brown and Hopkins (1450–1475)	Schumpeter-Gilboy (1700–1702)	Department of Employment (1967)	Composite Commodity Price Index (1860)
	1	2	3	4
1720	635	93.8		48.3
1721	604	91.9		46.0
1722	554	89.0		42.2
1723	525	85.1		40.0
1724	589	88.0		44.8
1725	610	89.5		46.4
1726	637	94.3		48.5
1727	596	93.8		45.4
1728	649	94.3		49.4
1729	681	96.8		51.8
1730	599	93.8		45.6
1731	553	89.0		42.1
1732	557	87.0		42.4
1733	544	83.1		41.4
1734	518	84.6		39.4
1735	529	83.6		40.3
1736	539	82.2		41.0
1737	581	84.6		44.2
1738	563	83.6		42.8
1739	547	85.6		41.6
1740	644	91.9		49.0
1741	712	99.7		54.2
1742	631	95.3		48.0
1743	579	90.0		44.1
1744	518	88.5		39.4
1745	528	80.7		40.2
1746	594	89.5		45.2
1747	574	85.6		43.7
1748	599	89.0		45.6
1749	609	90.9		46.4

Year (Base =)	Phelps Brown and Hopkins (1450–1475)	Schumpeter-Gilboy (1700–1702)	Department of Employment (1967)	Composite Commodity Price Index (1860)
	1	2	3	4
1750	590	89.0		44.9
1751	574	85.1		43.7
1752	601	84.6		45.7
1753	585	83.1		44.5
1754	615	87.0		46.8
1755	578	89.0		44.0
1756	602	90.0		45.8
1757	733	98.7		55.8
1758	731	100.6		55.6
1759	673	97.7		51.2
1760	643	97.2		48.9
1761	614	94.8		46.7
1762	638	95.3		48.6
1763	655	98.2		49.8
1764	713	98.7		54.3
1765	738	99.7		56.2
1766	747	100.2		56.8
1767	790	101.1		60.1
1768	781	100.2		59.4
1769	717	92.9		54.6
1770	714	94.3		54.3
1771	775	97.7		59.0
1772	858	104.5		65.3
1773	855	106.0		65.1
1774	863	104.1		65.7
1775	815	102.6		62.0
1776	797	104.5		60.6
1777	794	102.1		60.4
1778	826	107.5		62.9
1779	756	107.5		57.5

Year (Base =)	Phelps Brown and Hopkins (1450–1475)	Schumpeter-Gilboy (1700–1702)	Department of Employment (1967)	Composite Commodity Price Index (1860)
	1	2	3	4
1780	730	108.4		55.6
1781	760	109.4		57.8
1782	776	114.7		59.1
1783	869	119.6		66.1
1784	874	113.8		66.5
1785	839	110.4		63.8
1786	839	112.8		63.8
1787	834	110.9		63.5
1788	867	113.8		66.0
1789	856	108.9		65.1
1790	871	112.3		66.3
1791	870	110.9		66.2
1792	883	113.3		67.2
1793	908	123.0		69.1
1794	978	124.0		74.4
1795	1,091	130.8		83.0
1796	1,161	142.0		88.4
1797	1,045	140.5		79.5
1798	1,022	134.7		77.8
1799	1,148	144.4		87.4
1800	1,567	173.1		119.2
1801	1,751	189.6		133.3
1802	1,348			102.6
1803	1,268			96.5
1804	1,309			99.6
1805	1,521			115.8
1806	1,454			110.6
1807	1,427			108.6
1808	1,476			112.3
1809	1,619			123.2

Year (Base =)	Phelps Brown and Hopkins (1450–1475)	Schumpeter-Gilboy (1700–1702)	Department of Employment (1967)	Composite Commodity Price Index (1860)
	1	2	3	4
1810	1,670			127.1
1811	1,622			123.4
1812	1,836			139.7
1813	1,881			143.2
1814	1,642			125.0
1815	1,467			111.6
1816	1,344			202.3
1817	1,526			116.1
1818	1,530			116.4
1819	1,492			113.6
1820	1,353			103.0
1821	1,190			90.6
1822	1,029			78.3
1823	1,099			83.6
1824	1,193			90.8
1825	1,400			106.5
1826	1,323			100.7
1827	1,237			94.1
1828	1,201			91.4
1829	1,189			90.5
1830	1,146			87.2
1831	1,260			95.9
1832	1,167			88.8
1833	1,096			83.4
1834	1,011			76.9
1835	1,028			78.2
1836	1,141			86.8
1837	1,169			89.0
1838	1,177			89.6
1839	1,263			96.1

Year (Base =)	Phelps Brown and Hopkins (1450–1475)	Schumpeter-Gilboy (1700–1702)	Department of Employment (1967)	Composite Commodity Price Index (1860)
	1	2	3	4
1840	1,286			97.9
1841	1,256			95.6
1842	1,161			88.4
1843	1,030			78.4
1844	1,029			78.3
1845	1,079			82.1
1846	1,122			85.4
1847	1,257			95.7
1848	1,105			84.1
1849	1,035			78.8
1850	969			73.7
1851	961			73.1
1852	978			74.4
1853	1,135			86.4
1854	1,265			96.3
1855	1,274			97.0
1856	1,264			96.2
1857	1,287			97.9
1858	1,190			90.6
1859	1,214			92.4
1860	1,314			100.0
1861	1,302			99.1
1862	1,290			98.2
1863	1,144			87.1
1864	1,200			91.3
1865	1,238			94.2
1866	1,296			98.6
1867	1,346			102.4
1868	1,291			98.2
1869	1,244			94.7

Year (Base =)	Phelps Brown and Hopkins (1450–1475)	Schumpeter-Gilboy (1700–1702)	Department of Employment (1967)	Composite Commodity Price Index (1860)
	1	2	3	4
1870	1,241			94.4
1871	1,320			100.5
1872	1,378			104.9
1873	1,437			109.4
1874	1,423			108.3
1875	1,310			99.7
1876	1,370			104.3
1877	1,330			101.2
1878	1,281			97.5
1879	1,210			92.1
1880	1,174			89.3
1881	1,213			92.3
1882	1,140			86.8
1883	1,182			90.0
1884	1,071			81.5
1885	1,026			78.1
1886	931			70.8
1887	955			72.7
1888	950			72.3
1889	948			72.2
1890	947			72.1
1891	998			76.0
1892	996			75.8
1893	914			69.6
1894	982			74.7
1895	968			73.7
1896	947			72.1
1897	963			73.3
1898	982			74.7
1899	950			72.3

Year (Base =)	Phelps Brown and Hopkins (1450–1475)	Schumpeter-Gilboy (1700–1702)	Department of Employment (1967)	Composite Commodity Price Index (1860)
	1	2	3	4
1900	994			75.6
1901	986			75.0
1902	963			73.3
1903	1,004			76.4
1904	985			75.0
1905	989			75.3
1906	1,016			77.3
1907	1,031			78.5
1908	1,043			79.4
1909	1,058			80.5
1910	994			75.6
1911	984			74.9
1912	999			76.0
1913	1,021			77.7
1914	1,147			87.3
1915	1,317			100.2
1916	1,652			125.7
1917	1,965			149.5
1918	2,497			190.0
1919	2,254			171.5
1920	2,591			197.2
1921	2,048			155.9
1922	1,672			127.2
1923	1,726			131.4
1924	1,740			132.4
1925	1,708			130.0
1926	1,577			120.0
1927	1,496			113.8
1928	1,485			113.0
1929	1,511			115.0

Year (Base =)	Phelps Brown and Hopkins (1450–1475)	Schumpeter-Gilboy (1700–1702)	Department of Employment (1967)	Composite Commodity Price Index (1860)
	1	2	3	4
1930	1,275			97.0
1931	1,146			87.2
1932	1,065			81.0
1933	1,107			84.2
1934	1,097			83.5
1935	1,149			87.4
1936	1,211			92.2
1937	1,275			97.0
1938	1,274			97.0
1939	1,209			92.0
1940	1,574			119.8
1941	1,784			135.8
1942	2,130			162.1
1943	2,145			163.2
1944	2,216			168.6
1945	2,282			173.7
1946	2,364			179.9
1947	2,580			196.4
1948	2,781			211.6
1949	3,145			239.4
1950	3,155			240.1
1951	3,656			278.2
1952	3,987			303.4
1953	3,735			284.2
1954	3,825		68.9	291.1
1955			71.6	302.5
1956			73.9	312.2
1957			76.6	323.7
1958			78.9	333.3
1959			79.4	335.5

Year (Base =)	Phelps Brown and Hopkins (1450–1475)	Schumpeter–Gilboy (1700–1702)	Department of Employment (1967)	Composite Commodity Price Index (1860)
	1	2	3	4
1960			80.2	338.8
1961			82.9	350.2
1962			85.1	359.5
1963			86.8	366.7
1964			89.6	378.5
1965			93.9	396.7
1966			97.6	412.3
1967			100.0	422.5
1968			104.7	442.3
1969			110.4	466.4
1970			117.4	496.0
1971			128.5	542.9
1972			137.7	581.7
1973			150.2	634.6
1974			174.3	736.4
1975			216.5	914.7
1976			252.4	1,066.4
1977			291.4	1,231.1
1978			316.6	1,337.6
1979			359.0	1,516.7
1980			423.5	1,789.2
1981			473.8	2,001.8
1982			514.6	2,174.1
1983			538.2	2,273.8
1984			565.0	2,387.1
1985			599.4	2,532.4
1986			619.8	2,618.6
1987			645.7	2,727.8
1988			677.3	2,861.7
1989			729.9	3,083.8

Year (Base =)	Phelps Brown and Hopkins (1450–1475)	Schumpeter-Gilboy (1700–1702)	Department of Employment (1967)	Composite Commodity Price Index (1860)
	1	2	3	4
1990			799.0	3,375.6
1991			858.5	3,627.3
1992				
1993				

NOTES AND SOURCES: Dates in the table heading are the reference base periods (*e.g.*, 1451–75 = 100). The figures in Col. 1 are from E[rnest] H. Phelps Brown and Sheila V. Hopkins, 'Seven Centuries of the Prices of Consumables Compared with Builder's Wage-rates,' *Economica*, New Ser., XXIII (November 1956), 312–14. Col. 2 is the average of the two series developed and presented by Elizabeth Boody Schumpeter, 'English Prices and Public Finance, 1660–1822,' *Review of Economic Statistics*, XX (1938), 21–37, and Elizabeth W. Gilboy, 'The Cost of Living and Real Wages in Eighteenth Century England,' *Review of Economic Statistics*, XVIII (1936), 134–43. For Col. 3, see the text above and the sources cited in n. 43 especially [Great Britain, Central Statistical Office], *Annual Abstract of Statistics*, No. 125 (London: Her Majesty's Stationery Office, 1989), 316, and the mimeographed monthly updates issued by the Central Statistical Office titled 'Internal Purchasing Power of the Pound.' Col. 4 links Col. 1 and Col. 3 and converts them to the new base reference period (1860 = 100).

APPENDIX C

AMERICAN REVOLUTIONARY WAR CURRENCY DEPRECIATION TABLES

BECAUSE the depreciation in the purchasing power of the currency of the American Revolutionary War period was such a concern for contemporaries and because it is such a cause of confusion for historians, it is worth establishing the relationship between that currency and the commodity price index.

Just as they had done as colonies, during the American Revolutionary War period the various states of the United States issued paper money to be used as currency. So also did the central government, the Continental Congress.[46] The common unit of account for all these currencies was the dollar. Even though several of the states denominated their own paper monies in the old notation, all were established at a fixed, unvarying ratio to the new, national dollar.[47] At first the paper dollars of the Continental Congress and the states passed, as they were supposed to pass, as the equivalent to the coin after which they were named. One paper dollar was the same as one hard, silver dollar. That dollar, of course, was the Spanish piece of eight.

---

46. Studies of the money and finance of the period are numerous. Especially valuable is E[lmer] James Ferguson, *The Power of the Purse: A History of American Public Finance, 1776–1790* (Chapel Hill, North Carolina: University of North Carolina Press, 1961). See also Charles J. Bullock, *The Finances of the United States from 1775 to 1789, with Especial Reference to the Budget, Bulletin of the University of Wisconsin*, Economics, Political Science, and History Series, vol. 1, no. 2 (Madison, Wisconsin: The University, 1895), pp. 131–38.

Later, in the 1780s, some states also minted their own small denomination coins. See Eric P. Newman, 'Circulation of Pre-U.S. Mint Coppers,' in *America's Copper Coinage, 1783–1857* (New York: American Numismatic Society, 1984), pp. 101–16; and Philip L. Mossman, *Money of the American Colonies and Confederation: A Numismatic, Economic and Historical Correlation*, Numismatic Studies No. 20 (New York: American Numismatic Society, 1992).

47. These ratios were set out regularly in merchants' manuals and in newspapers. Thus, £100 currency in New England and Virginia were the equivalent of $333.33; in New York and North Carolina, $250.00; in New Jersey, Pennsylvania, Delaware, and Maryland, $266.67; in South Carolina and Georgia, $428.57. See, e.g., Samuel Freeman, *A Valuable Assistant to Every Man: or, the American Clerk's Magazine*, 2d ed. (Boston, Massachusetts: I[saiah] Thomas and E[benezer] T. Andrews, 1795), pp. 229–34. Compare Nicholas Pike, *A New and Complete System of Arithmetic, Composed for the Use of the Citizens of the United States*, [1st ed.] (Newburyport, Massachusetts: John Mycall, 1788), pp. 376–78; and Joseph Chaplin, *The Trader's Best Companion: Containing Various Arithmetical Rules . . . Applied to the Federal Currency . . .* (Newburyport, Massachusetts: William Barrett, 1795), pp. 3, 32.

The problems of war soon changed all that. Paper money began to lose its worth; people came to value it less than they valued the silver dollar. Everyone quickly learned to demand and to pay more in paper currency than they did in hard currency. What cost $2.00 if you paid in silver, cost $3.00 and then $4.00 if you tried to pay with paper money. As the gap between the two widened, it became increasingly necessary to specify and to record the difference. So much was the paper money issued by the Continental Congress (the 'Continentals') found to be unacceptable that people rarely used it for accounting purposes and preferred instead to continue to price goods and services either in hard silver dollars or in their old colonial moneys of account.[48] Compounding the consequent difficulties, each state's paper money behaved somewhat differently from that issued by its neighbors and from Congress's 'Continentals'. As confusion bred chaos, Congress finally acted and declared that, as of mid-March 1780, the old paper money would no longer be recognized as legal tender currency in the country. While some of it continued to circulate in daily transactions—and indeed continued in some places to depreciate in its worth, after mid-1780 prices and wages could legally be expressed only in the new United States dollars.[49]

The data in Table C-1 and Table C-2 replicate contemporary tables of the depreciation of the wartime paper money against silver dollars.[50]

48. Winifred B. Rothenberg, 'The Emergence of a Capital Market in Rural Massachusetts, 1780–1838,' *Journal of Economic History*, XLV (December 1985), 808.

49. For a contemporary account of what happened, see the letter of Gouverneur Morris to the unofficial agent in the United States of the government of Spain, Francisco Rendón, dated at Philadelphia, March 5, 1782, in *The Papers of Robert Morris, 1781–1784*, edited by E[lmer] James Ferguson, *et al.*, 7 vols. (Pittsburgh, 1973 to date), IV, 352–58, and the report Rendón wrote based in large part on Morris's letter, dated Philadelphia, April 20, 1782, in *ibid.*, pp. 595–624. For an important perspective on all this, see Charles W. Calomiris, 'Institutional Failure, Monetary Scarcity, and the Depreciation of the Continental,' *Journal of Economic History*, XLVIII (March 1988), 47–68. Compare Ron Michener, 'Backing Theories and the Currencies of Eighteenth-Century America,' *ibid.*, XLVIII (September 1988), 682–92; and Calomiris, 'The Depreciation of the Continental: A Reply,' *ibid.*, pp. 693–98.

50. Compare Bullock, *Finances of the United States*, p. 133; and Bezanson *et al.*, *Prices and Inflation during the American Revolution*, pp. 58–72 *et passim*. Ferguson, *Power of the Purse*, pp. 68–69, made the valid point that these official tables of depreciation understated the full extent of paper money's loss of purchasing power. But compare Pelatiah Webster, *Political Essays on the Nature and Operation of Money, Public Finances, and Other Subjects: Published during the American War, and Continued to the Present Year, 1791* (Philadelphia, Pennsylvania: Joseph Crukshank, 1791), pp. 501–02. In part to offset this problem, the state governments of Massachusetts and South Carolina established rates of depreciation using indexes of commodity prices (see n. 7, above).

For instance, according to these tables, by December 1778, it took 600 Pennsylvania paper dollars or 681 Continental paper dollars to buy what was worth 100 silver dollars. Recall that the fluctuations recorded in the commodity price index in Table A-2, Col. 6, are expressed in hard dollars. Thus it is necessary to convert a sum stated in Pennsylvania paper money (or any of the other paper monies in use at the time) to silver dollars using Table C-1 before reducing it to any constant value using the commodity price index in Table A-2.

TABLE C-1

AMERICAN REVOLUTIONARY WAR CURRENCY
DEPRECIATION TABLES

Year Month	Continental Currency	Massachusetts New Hampshire Rhode Island Currency	New York Connecticut Currency	Pennsylvania Delaware Currency	New Jersey Currency
	1	2	3	4	5
January 1777	100	105	100	150	120
February	100	107	100	150	195
March	100	109	100	200	210
April	100	112	100	250	310
May	100	115	100	250	410
June	100	120	100	250	200
July	100	125	100	300	225
August	100	150	100	300	250
September	104	175	102	300	275
October	115	275	112	300	300
November	126	300	124	300	300
December	138	310	136	400	300
January 1778	152	325	149	400	400
February	168	350	164	500	400
March	186	375	181	500	400
April	214	400	209	600	500
May	245	400	238	500	500
June	282	400	273	400	500
July	322	425	318	400	500
August	371	450	359	500	500
September	429	475	415	500	500
October	500	500	482	500	500
November	585	545	565	600	600
December	681	634	655	600	700
January 1779	796	742	769	800	800
February	932	868	909	1,000	1,000
March	1,046	1,000	1,024	1,050	1,200

Year Month	Continental Currency	Massachusetts New Hampshire Rhode Island Currency	New York Connecticut Currency	Pennsylvania Delaware Currency	New Jersey Currency
	1	2	3	4	5
April	1,159	1,104	1,130	1,700	1,600
May	1,271	1,215	1,246	2,400	2,000
June	1,403	1,342	1,374	2,000	2,000
July	1,544	1,477	1,517	1,900	2,000
August	1,705	1,630	1,670	2,000	2,400
September	1,904	1,800	2,021	2,400	2,400
October	2,147	2,030	2,142	3,000	3,000
November	2,432	2,308	2,387	3,850	3,600
December	2,744	2,593	2,669	4,150	4,000
January 1780	3,107	2,934	3,024	4,050	4,200
February	3,519	3,322	3,433	4,750	5,000
March	3,954	3,736	3,866	6,150	6,000
April	4,000	4,200		6,150	6,000
May		5,300		5,900	6,000
June		6,700		6,150	6,000
July		6,950		6,450	6,000
August		7,000		7,000	6,000
September		7,100		7,200	6,000
October		7,200		7,200	7,500
November		7,300		7,400	7,500
December		7,433		7,500	7,500
January 1781		7,467		7,500	7,500
February		7,500		7,500	9,000
March		8,000		12,500	10,000
April		8,500		16,000	12,000
May		9,000		22,500	15,000
June		10,000			
July					
August					
September					
October					
November					
December					

TABLE C-2

AMERICAN REVOLUTIONARY WAR CURRENCY
DEPRECIATION TABLES

Year Month	Maryland Currency	Virginia Currency	North Carolina Currency	South Carolina Currency
	1	2	3	4
January 1777	150	150	100	100
February	150	150	100	100
March	200	200	125	100
April	250	250	150	108
May	250	250	150	117
June	250	250	175	125
July	300	300	200	139
August	300	300	213	152
September	300	300	225	166
October	300	300	250	186
November	300	300	250	206
December	400	400	300	226
January 1778	400	400	350	221
February	500	500	350	211
March	500	500	375	267
April	600	500	400	317
May	500	500	400	328
June	400	500	400	347
July	400	500	400	354
August	500	500	425	361
September	500	500	450	380
October	500	500	475	405
November	600	600	500	520
December	600	600	550	629
January 1779	800	800	600	761
February	1,000	1,000	650	832

Year Month	Maryland Currency	Virginia Currency	North Carolina Currency	South Carolina Currency
	1	2	3	4
March	1,000	1,000	750	893
April	1,700	1,600	1,000	966
May	2,400	2,000	1,000	832
June	2,000	2,000	1,225	1,177
July	2,000	2,100	1,500	1,457
August	2,000	2,200	1,800	1,637
September	2,400	2,400	2,100	1,618
October	3,000	2,800	2,500	2,040
November	3,850	3,600	2,700	2,596
December	4,150	4,000	3,000	3,233
January 1780	4,000	4,200	3,200	3,775
February	4,700	4,500	3,500	4,217
March	6,000	5,000	4,000	4,659
April	6,000	6,000	5,000	5,101
May	6,000	6,000	6,000	5,245
June	6,000	6,500	7,500	
July	6,000	6,500	9,000	
August	6,500	7,000	10,000	
September	7,500	7,200	12,500	
October	8,500	7,300	15,000	
November	9,000	7,400	17,500	
December	10,000	7,500	20,000	
January 1781	11,000	7,500	21,000	
February	12,000	8,000	22,500	
March	14,000	9,000	25,000	
April	16,000	10,000	26,000	
May	28,000	15,000	30,000	
June	28,000	25,000	35,000	
July		40,000	40,000	
August		50,000	50,000	
September		60,000	55,000	

Year Month	Maryland Currency	Virginia Currency	North Carolina Currency	South Carolina Currency
	1	2	3	4
October		70,000	60,000	
November		80,000	67,500	
December		100,000	72,500	

NOTES AND SOURCES: The data are as published in [United States, Congress], *American State Papers: Documents, Legislative and Executive, of the Congress of the United States*, 38 vols. (Washington, D.C.: Gales and Seaton, 1832–61), Class III: *Finance*, V, 766–74. Compare Henry Phillips, Jr., *Historical Sketches of the Paper Currency of the American Colonies, prior to the Adoption of the Federal Constitution*, 2 vols. (Roxbury, Massachusetts: W. Elliot Woodward, 1865), II, 206–18. The value for Continental currency is that for the 15th of each month; the value for New York currency is the mean of the values given. A few of the values for Massachusetts currency are straight-line interpolations based on data for the neighboring months; they are italicized. Compare, also, Pelatiah Webster, *Political Essays on the Nature and Operation of Money, Public Finances, and Other Subjects: Published during the American War, and Continued to the Present Year, 1791* (Philadelphia, Pennsylvania: Joseph Crukshank, 1791), pp. 501–02.

APPENDIX D

PERIODS OF EXPANSION AND CONTRACTION IN THE ECONOMY OF EARLY AMERICA, 1701–1838

COMMODITY PRICE DATA may be used to help identify the phases of the business cycle, at least up to the beginning of the Second World War, as was discussed above. The index numbers in Table A-2, Col. 6, for the eighteenth century and early nineteenth century are the basis of both Table D-1 and Figure 1. Between 1701 and 1836 there were twenty-four full cycles of contraction and expansion. The average cycle lasted just over five-and-a-half years, peak to peak.[51] The trend line over the eighteenth century indicates, first, a long-term decline that had its beginnings in the seventeenth century and reached its nadir during the 1730s; and, second, a subsequent steady rise that continued on into the nineteenth century. Both the fluctuations and the trends in the business cycle of the early American economy were paralleled by the fluctuations and trends in the economy of Great Britain (see Appendix B).[52]

51. Between 1836 and 1990, the economy of the United States experienced thirty-five cycles that averaged, peak to peak, over fifty-three months in duration according to the National Bureau of Economic Research. Burns and Mitchell, *Measuring Business Cycles*, p. 78; *Statistical Abstract of the United States*, 109th ed. (1989), p. 534; 'Business Cycle Expansions and Contractions in the United States,' *Business Conditions Digest*, 30 (Jan. 1990), 104. The most recent peak was in July 1990.

52. See, again, McCusker and Menard, *Economy of British America*, pp. 62–64, Table 3.4. Compare, for instance, J[onathan] R. T. Hughes and Nathan Rosenberg, 'The United States Business Cycle before 1860: Some Problems of Interpretation,' *Economic History Review*, 2d Ser., xv (December 1963), 481, 493, and the works they cite, R[obert] C. O. Matthews, *A Study in Trade-Cycle History: Economic Fluctuations in Great Britain, 1833–1842* (Cambridge: University Press, 1954), pp. 43–69, 202–24 *et passim*; J[onathan] R. T. Hughes, *Fluctuations in Trade, Industry, and Finance* (Oxford: Clarendon Press, 1960), p. 40. See also W[alt] W. Rostow, *The World Economy: History & Prospect* (Austin, Texas: University of Texas Press, [1978]), pp. 311, 315 *et passim*.

Table D-1

PERIODS OF EXPANSION AND CONTRACTION IN THE ECONOMY OF EARLY AMERICA 1701–1838

Dates of Peaks and Troughs by Calendar Years		Length of Cycle	
Trough	Peak	Trough to Trough	Peak to Peak
	1701		
1705	1708		7
1710	1713	5	5
1716	1719	6	6
1721	1725	5	6
1733	1738	12	13
1739	1741	6	3
1745	1749	6	8
1750	1752	5	3
1756	1759	6	7
1764	1766	8	7
1768	1770	4	4
1771	1772	3	2
1775	1778	4	6
1779	1780	4	2
1781	1782	2	2
1789	1796	8	14
1798	1801	9	5
1802	1806	4	5
1807	1808	5	2
1810	1814	3	6
1818	1819	8	5
1821	1822	3	3
1824	1827	3	5
1834	1836	10	9
1838		4	

NOTES AND SOURCES: The periods are as indicated in Table A-2, Col. 6. In some instances, they modify the beginning or the ending of the periods set out in a similar attempt. in John J. McCusker and Russell R. Menard, *The Economy of British America, 1607–1789* (Chapel Hill, North Carolina: University of North Carolina Press, 1985), pp. 62–63, Table 3.4. In some instances short cycles identified there have been merged here either because of the availability of better data or because, in a reinterpretation of the data, an intervening period seems not to have been important statistically or historically. Compare Figure 1.

LIST OF SOURCES

MANUSCRIPTS

William Beveridge Papers, Wages and Prices Collection, Manuscript Department, British Library of Political and Economic Science, London School of Economics and Political Science

Collectie Commerciële Couranten, 15e–19e Eeuw, Economisch-Historische Bibliotheek, Amsterdam

Frank Ashmore Pearson Papers, Albert R. Mann Library, Cornell University, Ithaca, New York

'(Industrial Research Department), Wholesale Prices' Collection, Wharton School of Finance and Commerce, University of Pennsylvania, Philadelphia, Pennsylvania

Records of the International Scientific Committee on Price History, 1928–39, Manuscript and Archives Division, Baker Library, Graduate School of Business Administration, Harvard University, Boston, Massachusetts

PRINTED MATERIALS

Adams, Donald R., Jr. 'One Hundred Years of Prices and Wages: Maryland, 1750–1850,' *Working Papers from the Regional Economic History Research Center*, v (No. 4, 1985), 90–129

—— 'Prices and Wages,' in *Encyclopaedia of American Economic History: Studies of the Principal Movements and Ideas*, edited by [Patrick] Glenn Porter, 3 vols. (New York: Charles Scribner's Sons, 1980), I, 229–46

—— 'Prices and Wages in Maryland, 1750–1850,' *Journal of Economic History*, XLVI (September 1986), 625–45

—— 'Wage Rates in the Early National Period: Philadelphia, 1785–1830,' *Journal of Economic History*, XXVI (September 1968), 404–26

America's Copper Coinage, 1783–1857 (New York: American Numismatic Society, 1984)

The American Business Cycle: Continuity and Change, edited by Robert J. Gordon, National Bureau of Economic Research, *Studies in Business Cycles*, Vol. 25 (Chicago: University of Chicago Press, 1986)

Anderson, Terry Lee. *The Economic Growth of Seventeenth Century New England: A Measurement of Regional Income* ([Ph.D. dissertation, University of Washington, 1972]; New York: Arno Press, 1975)

—— 'Wealth Estimates for the New England Colonies, 1650–1709,' *Explorations in Economic History*, XII (April 1975), 151–76

Berry, Thomas Senior. *Western Prices before 1861: A Study of the Cincinnati Market*, Harvard Economic Studies, Vol. LXXIV (Cambridge, Massachusetts: Harvard University Press, 1943)

Beveridge, William [Henry]. *Prices and Wages in England from the Twelfth to the Nineteenth Century* (London: Longmans Green and Co., 1939)

Bezanson, Anne, Blanch Daley, Marjorie C. Denison and Miriam Hussey. *Prices and Inflation during the American Revolution: Pennsylvania, 1770–1790* (Philadelphia, Pennsylvania: University of Pennsylvania Press, 1951)

Bezanson, Anne, Robert D. Gray, and Miriam Hussey. *Prices in Colonial Pennsylvania* (Philadelphia, Pennsylvania: University of Pennsylvania Press. 1935)

Boorsma, Peter, and Joost van Genabeek. *Commercial and Financial Serial Publications of the Netherlands Economic History Archives: Commodity Price Currents, Foreign Exchange Rate Currents, Stock Exchange Rate Currents and Auction Lists, 1580–1870*. Nederlandsch Economisch-Historisch Archief, Inventarisatie Bijzondere Collecties 4 (Amsterdam: Nederlandsch Economisch-Historisch Archief, 1991)

Bordo, Michael D., and Anna J. Schwartz. 'Money and Prices in the 19th Century: Was Thomas Tooke Right?' *Explorations in Economic History*. XVIII (April 1981), 97–127

Brock, Leslie V. *The Currency of the American Colonies, 1700–1764: A Study in Colonial Finance and Imperial Relations* ([Ph.D. dissertation, University of Michigan. 1941]; New York: Arno Press, 1975)

Bullock, Charles J. *The Finances of the United States from 1755 to 1789, with Especial Reference to the Budget, Bulletin of the University of Wisconsin*, Bulletin of the University of Wisconsin, Economics, Political Science, and History Series, vol. 1, no. 2 (Madison, Wisconsin: The University, 1895)

Burns, Arthur F., and Wesley C. Mitchell. *Measuring Business Cycles*, National Bureau of Economic Research, Studies in Business Cycles, Vol. 2 (New York: National Bureau of Economic Research, 1946)

'Business Cycle Expansions and Contractions in the United States,' *Business Conditions Digest*, 30 (January 1990), 104

Calomiris, Charles W. 'The Depreciation of the Continental: A Reply,' *Journal of Economic History*, XLVIII (September 1988), pp. 693–98

—— 'Institutional Failure, Monetary Scarcity, and the Depreciation of the Continental,' *Journal of Economic History*, XLVIII (March 1988), 47–68

Carli, Gian Rinaldo. *Delle Monete e dell'Instituzione delle Zecche d'Italia, dell'Antico, e Presente Sistema d'Esse e del loro intrinseco Valore, e Rapporto con la Presente Moneta dalla Decadenza dell'Imperio sino Secolo XVII*, 4 vols. in 3 (Mantua: [n. p.], 1754; Pisa: Giovan Paolo Giovannelli, e Compagni, 1757; and Luccca: Jacopo Giusti, 1760)

Chaplin, Joseph. *The Trader's Best Companion: Containing Various Arithmetical Rules ... Applied to the Federal Currency ...* (Newburyport, Massachusetts: William Barrett, 1795)

Chaudhuri, K. N. *The Trading World of Asia and the English East India Company, 1660–1760* (Cambridge: Cambridge University Press, 1978)

Clark, G[eorge] N. 'The Occasion of Fleetwood's "Chronicon Preciosum",' *English Historical Review*, LI (October 1936), 686–90

[Cochran, Thomas C.] 'A Survey of Concepts and Viewpoints in the Social Sciences,' *The Social Sciences in Historical Study: A Report of the Committee on Historiography*, [edited by Hugh G. J. Aitken], Social Science Research Council, Bulletin 64 (New York: Social Science Research Council, 1965), pp. 34–85

Cole, Arthur Harrison. *Wholesale Commodity Prices in the United States, 1700–1861*, 2 vols. (Cambridge, Massachusetts: Harvard University Press, 1938)

Cole, Arthur H., and Ruth Crandall. 'The International Scientific Committee on Price History,' *Journal of Economic History*, XXIV (September 1964), 381–88

Coquelin, Ch[arles], and [Gilbert Urbain] Guillaumin. *Dictionnaire de l'économie politique*, 2d ed., 2 vols. (Paris: Guillaumin & Cie., 1854)

Craven, B. M., and R. Gausden. 'How Best to Measure Inflation? The UK and Europe,' *The Royal Bank of Scotland Review*, No. 170 (June 1991), 26–37

Crowe, Walter R. *Index Numbers: Theory and Application* (London: Macdonald & Evans Ltd., 1965)

David, Paul A., and Peter Solar. 'A Bicentenary Contribution to the History of the Cost of Living in America,' *Research in Economic History*, II (1977), 1–80

Davis, Ralph. *The Industrial Revolution and British Overseas Trade* (Leicester: Leicester University Press, 1979)

Davisson, William I. 'Essex County Price Trends: Money and Markets in 17th Century Massachusetts,' *Essex Institute Historical Collections*, CIII (April 1967), 141–85

Deane, Phyllis, and W[illiam] A. Cole. *British Economic Growth, 1688–1959: Trends and Structure*, 2d ed. (Cambridge: Cambridge University Press, 1969)

De Roover, Raymond [A.] *The Medici Bank: Its Organization, Management, Operations, and Decline* (New York: New York University Press, 1948)

Diewert, W[alter] E. 'Index Number,' in *The New Palgrave: A Dictionary of Economics*, edited by John Eatwell, Murray Milgate, and Peter Newman, 4 vols. (London: The Macmillan Press Ltd., 1987) II, 767–80

[Dutot, Charles de Ferrare.] *Réflexions politiques sur les finances et le commerce. Où l'on examine quelles ont été sur les revenus, les denrées, le change étranger, & conséquemment sur notre commerce, les influences des augmentations et les diminutions des valeurs numéraires des monnoyes*, 2 vols. (The Hague: V[aillant] and N[icolas] Prevost, 1738)

Eichhorn, Wolfgang. *Measurement in Economics: Theory and Application of Economic Indices* (Heidelberg: Physica-Verlag, 1988)

Encyclopædia of American Economic History: Studies of the Principal Movements and Ideas, edited by [Patrick] Glenn Porter, 3 vols. (New York: Charles Scribner's Sons, 1980)

Falla, G. A. *A Catalogue of the Papers of William Henry Beveridge, 1st Baron Beveridge* ([London:] British Library of Political and Economic Science, 1981)

Faulkner, Harold Underwood. *American Economic History*, revised by Harry N. Scheiber and Harold G. Vatter, 9th ed. (New York: Harper & Row, [1976])

Ferguson, E[lmer] James. *The Power of the Purse: A History of American Public Finance, 1776–1790* (Chapel Hill, North Carolina: University of North Carolina Press, 1961)

Fisher, Franklin M., and Karl Shell. 'Taste and Quality Change in the Pure Theory of the True Cost-of-Living Index,' in *Value, Capital, and Growth: Papers in Honour of Sir John Hicks*, edited by J[ames] N. Wolfe (Edinburgh: Edinburgh University Press, 1967), pp. 97–139

Fisher, Irving. *The Making of Index Numbers: A Study of Their Varieties, Tests, and Reliability*, 3rd ed., rev. (Boston, Massachusetts: Houghton Mifflin Co., 1927)

Fisher, Willard C. 'The Tabular Standard in Massachusetts History,' *Quarterly Journal of Economics*, XXVII (May 1913), 417–51

Fite, Gilbert C., and Jim E. Reese. *An Economic History of the United States*, 3rd ed. (Boston, Massachusetts: Houghton Mifflin Co., 1973)

[Fitzpatrick, F. A.] *Wholesale Price Index: Principles and Procedures*, Studies in Official Statistics No. 32 (London: Her Majesty's Stationery Office, [1980].)

Fleetwood, [William]. *Chronicon Preciosum: or, An Account of English Gold and Silver Money, the Price of Corn, and Other Commodities, ... &c. in England, for Six Hundred Years Last Past*, [rev. ed.] (London: T[homas] Osborne, 1745)

Flinn, M[ichael] W. 'Trends in Real Wages, 1750–1850,' *Economic History Review*, 2d Ser., XXVII (August 1974), 399–413

Fogel, Robert William. *Without Consent or Contract: The Rise and Fall of American Slavery* (New York: W. W. Norton & Company, 1989)

Fowler, R[onald] F. *Some Problems of Index Number Construction*, Studies in Official Statistics, Research Series, No. 3 (London: Her Majesty's Stationery Office, 1970)

Fourastié, Jacqueline. *Les formules d'indices de prix: Calculs numériques et commentaires théoriques* (Paris: Librairie Armand Colin, 1966)

[Franklin, Benjamin]. *A Modest Inquiry into the Nature and Necessity of a Paper-Currency* (Philadelphia, Pennsylvania: New Printing Office, 1729)

—— *The Papers of Benjamin Franklin*, edited by Leonard W. Labaree *et al.* (New Haven, Connecticut: Yale University, 1959 to date)

Freeman, Samuel. *A Valuable Assistant to Every Man: or, the American Clerk's Magazine*, 2d ed. (Boston, Massachusetts: I[saiah] Thomas and E[benezer] T. Andrews, 1795)

Gallman, Robert E. 'Comment,' *Journal of Economic History*, XXXIX (March 1979), 311–12

Gilboy, Elizabeth W. 'The Cost of Living and Real Wages in Eighteenth Century England,' *Review of Economic Statistics*, XVIII (1936), 134–43

Gordon, Donald F. 'Value, Labor Theory of,' in *International Encyclopedia of the Social Sciences*, edited by David L. Sills, 17 vols. ([New York:] The Macmillan Company & The Free Press, [1968]), XVI, 279–83

[Great Britain. Central Statistical Office]. *Annual Abstract of Statistics*, No. 125 (London: Her Majesty's Stationery Office, 1989)

—— *Monthly Digest of Statistics* (monthly since 1980)

Gunnarsson, Gisli. 'A Study in the Historiography of Prices,' *Economy and History*, XIX (1976), 124–41

Gwyn, Julian. 'British Government Spending and the North American Colonies, 1740–1775,' *Journal of Imperial and Commonwealth History*, VIII (January 1980), 74–84

Hall, Thomas E. *Business Cycles: The Nature and Causes of Economic Fluctuations* (New York: Praeger Publishers, 1990)

Hamilton, Earl J. 'Prices, Wages, and the Industrial Revolution,' in *Studies in Economics and Industrial Relations*, by Wesley C. Mitchell *et al.* (Philadelphia, Pennsylvania: University of Pennsylvania Press, 1941), pp. 99–112

—— 'Use and Misuse of Price History,' in *The Tasks of Economic History: Papers Presented at the Fourth Annual Meeting of the Economic History Association—A Supplemental Issue of the Journal of Economic History*, [Supplement IV] (New York, 1944), pp. 47–60

—— *War and Prices in Spain, 1651–1800*, Harvard Economic Studies, Vol. LXXXI (Cambridge, Massachusetts: Harvard University Press, 1947)

Hughes, Jonathan [R. T.] *American Economic History*, 3d ed. (Glenview, Illinois: Scott, Foresman and Co., 1990)

—— *Fluctuations in Trade, Industry, and Finance* (Oxford: Clarendon Press, 1960)

Hughes, Jonathan [R. T.], and Nathan Rosenberg. 'The United States Business Cycle before 1860: Some Problems of Interpretation,' *Economic History Review*, 2d Ser., XV (December 1963), 476–93

Hutchison, Terence [W.] *Before Adam Smith: The Emergence of Political Economy, 1662–1776* (Oxford: Basil Blackwell, [1988])

International Encyclopedia of the Social Sciences, edited by David L. Sills, 17 vols. ([New York:] The Macmillan Company & The Free Press, [1968])

International Monetary Fund. *International Financial Statistics* (monthly since 1947)

Inventaires après-décès et ventes de meubles: Rapports à une histoire de la vie économique et quotidienne (XIVᵉ–XIXᵉ siècles), edited by Micheline Baulant, Anton J. Schuurman, and Paul Servais, Actes du Séminaire Tenu dans le Cadre du 9ème Congrès International d'Histoire Économique de Berne (Louvain-la-Neuve, Belgium: Academia, 1988)

Jastram, Roy W. *The Golden Constant: The English and American Experience, 1560–1976* (New York: John Wiley & Sons, [1977])

—— *Silver: The Restless Metal* (New York: John Wiley & Sons, [1981])

Jones, Alice Hanson. *American Colonial Wealth: Documents and Methods*, 2d ed., 3 vols. (New York: Arno Press, 1978)

—— *American Colonial Wealth: Documents and Methods for the American Middle Colonies, 1774*, separate number of *Economic Development and Cultural Change*, XVIII (July 1970)

Kravis, Irving B. 'Comparative Studies of National Incomes and Prices,' *Journal of Economic Literature*, XXII (March 1984), 1–39

Kydland, Finn E., and Edward C. Prescott. 'Business Cycles: Real Facts and a Monetary Myth,' *Federal Reserve Bank of Minneapolis Quarterly Review*, XIV (Spring 1990), 3–18

Lebergott, Stanley. *Manpower in Economic Growth: The American Record since 1800* (New York: McGraw-Hill Book Company, 1964)

—— 'Wage Trends, 1800–1900,' in *Trends in the American Economy in the Nineteenth Century*, edited by William N. Parker, National Bureau of Economic Research, Studies in Income and Wealth, Vol. 24 (Princeton, New Jersey: Princeton University Press, 1960), pp. 449–99

Lindert, Peter H. 'Probates, Prices, and Preindustrial Living Standards,' in *Inventaires après-décès et ventes de meubles: Rapports à une histoire de la vie économique et quotidienne (XIVe–XIXe siècles)*, edited by Micheline Baulant, Anton J. Schuurman, and Paul Servais (Louvain-la-Neuve, Belgium: Academia, 1987), pp. 171–80

Loschky, D[avid] [J.] 'Seven Centuries of Real Income per Wage Earner Reconsidered,' *Economica*, New Ser., XLVII (November 1980), 459–65

Lucas, Robert E., Jr. 'Understanding Business Cycles,' in *Stabilization of the Domestic and International Economy*, edited by Karl Brunner and Allan H. Meltzer, Carnegie-Rochester Conference Series on Public Policy, Vol. 5 (Amsterdam: North-Holland Publishing Company, 1977), pp. 7–29

Lydall, H[arold] F., and E[rnest] H. Phelps Brown. 'Seven Centuries of Real Income per Wage-Earner Reconsidered: A Note,' *Economica*, New Ser., XLIX (May 1982), 201–05

McCusker, John J. 'The Current Value of English Exports, 1697 to 1800,' *William and Mary Quarterly*, 3d Ser., XXVIII (October 1971), 607–28

—— *Money and Exchange in Europe and America, 1600–1775: A Handbook* (Chapel Hill, North Carolina: University of North Carolina Press, and London: The Macmillan Press Ltd., 1978)

—— *Rum and the American Revolution: The Rum Trade and the Balance of Payments of the Thirteen Continental Colonies* ([Ph.D. dissertation, University of Pittsburgh, 1970]; New York: Garland Publishing Inc., 1989)

McCusker, John J., and Russell R. Menard. *The Economy of British America, 1607–1789* (Chapel Hill, North Carolina: University of North Carolina Press, 1985)

Marx, Karl. *Capital: A Critique of Political Economy*, edited by Friedrich Engels, translated and edited by Samuel Moore and Edward Aveling, revised by Ernest Untermann, 3 vols. (1867–94; Chicago: Charles H. Kerr and Co., 1906–09)

[Massachusetts (Colony), Laws, statutes, etc.] *The Acts and Resolves, Public and Private, of the Province of the Massachusetts Bay,* [ed. Abner Cheney Goodell *et al.*], 21 vols. (Boston, Massachusetts: Wright and Porter, 1869–1922)

Matthews, R[obert] C. O. *A Study in Trade-Cycle History: Economic Fluctuations in Great Britain, 1833–1842* (Cambridge: University Press, 1954)

Meek, Ronald L. *Smith, Marx, & After: Ten Essays in the Development of Economic Thought* (London: Chapman & Hall, 1977)

—— *Studies in the Labour Theory of Value*, 2d ed. (London: Lawrence & Wishart, 1973)

Michener, Ron. 'Backing Theories and the Currencies of Eighteenth-Century America,' *Journal of Economic History*, XLVIII (September 1988), 682–92

Mitchell, Brian R. *British Historical Statistics* (Cambridge: Cambridge University Press, 1988)

Mitchell, Wesley C. 'The Making and Using of Index Numbers,' in [United States, Department of Labor, Bureau of Labor Statistics], *Index Numbers of Wholesale Prices in the United States and Foreign Countries*, Bureau of Labor Statistics, Bulletin No. 284 (Washington, D.C.: United States Government Printing Office, 1921)

Moore, Geoffrey H. 'A Truism: Recession Slows Inflation,' *New York Times*, Sunday, November 18, 1979, Business and Finance section

Morris, Richard B., ed. *Encyclopedia of American History*, rev. ed. (New York: Harper & Row, 1965)

[Morris, Robert]. *The Papers of Robert Morris, 1781–1784*, edited by E[lmer] James Ferguson, *et al.*, 7 vols. (Pittsburgh, 1973 to date)

Mossman, Philip L. *Money of the American Colonies and Confederation: A Numismatic, Economic and Historical Correlation*, Numismatic Studies No. 20 (New York: American Numismatic Society, 1992)

Mudgett, Bruce D. *Index Numbers* (New York: John Wiley & Sons, 1951)

Newman, Eric P. 'Circulation of Pre-U.S. Mint Coppers,' in *America's Copper Coinage, 1783–1857* (New York: American Numismatic Society, 1984), pp. 101–16

The New Palgrave: A Dictionary of Economics, edited by John Eatwell, Murray Milgate, and Peter Newman, 4 vols. (London: The Macmillan Press Ltd., 1987)

Oldham, James C. 'The Origins of the Special Jury,' *University of Chicago Law Review*, L (Winter 1983), 144–50

[Petty, William]. *A Treatise of Taxes & Contributions: Shewing the Nature and Measures of Crown-Lands* ... (London: N[athaniel] Brooke, 1662)

Phelps Brown, [Ernest] Henry. 'Gregory King's Notebook and the Phelps Brown-Hopkins Price Index,' *Economic History Review*, 2d Ser., XLIII (February 1990), 99–103

Phelps Brown, E[rnest] H., and Sheila V. Hopkins. *A Perspective of Wages and Prices* (London and New York: Methuen, 1981)

—— 'Seven Centuries of the Prices of Consumables Compared with Builders' Wage-rates,' *Economica*, New Ser., XXIII (November 1956), 296–314

Phillips, Henry, Jr. *Historical Sketches of the Paper Currency of the American Colonies, prior to the Adoption of the Federal Constitution*, 2 vols. (Roxbury, Massachusetts: W. Elliot Woodward, 1865)

Pike, Nicholas. *A New and Complete System of Arithmetic, Composed for the Use of the Citizens of the United States*, [1st ed.] (Newburyport, Massachusetts: John Mycall, 1788)

Pollak, Robert A. *The Theory of the Cost-of-Living Index* (New York: Oxford University Press, 1989)

Posthumus, N[icolaas] W. *Nederlandsche Prijsgeschiedenis*, 2 vols. (Leiden: E. J. Brill, 1943–64)

I Prezzi in Europa del XIII Secolo a Oggi, edited by Ruggiero Romano ([Turin]: Giulio Einaudi, [1967])

Price Indexes and Quality Change: Studies in New Methods of Measurement, edited by Zvi Griliches (Cambridge, Massachusetts: Harvard University Press, 1971)

Reitlinger, Gerald. *The Economics of Taste*, 3 vols. (London: Barrie and Rockliff, 1961–70)

Rostow, W[alt] W. *The World Economy: History & Prospect* (Austin, Texas: University of Texas Press, [1978])

Rostow, W[alt] W., and Michael Kennedy. 'A Simple Model of the Kondratieff Cycle,' *Research in Economic History*, IV (1979), 1–36

Rothenberg, Winifred B. 'The Emergence of a Capital Market in Rural Massachusetts, 1780–1838,' *Journal of Economic History*, 45 (1985), 808

—— 'A Price Index for Rural Massachusetts, 1750–1855.' *Journal of Economic History*, XXXIX (December 1979), 975–1001

Ruist, Erik, Ethel D. Hoover, and Philip J. McCarthy. 'Index Numbers,' *International Encyclopedia of the Social Sciences*, edited by David L. Sills, 17 vols. ([New York:] The Macmillan Company & The Free Press, [1968]), VII, 154–69

Schumpeter, Elizabeth Boody. 'English Prices and Public Finance, 1660–1822,' *Review of Economic Statistics*, XX (1938), 21–37

Smith, Adam. *An Inquiry into the Nature and Causes of the Wealth of Nations* (1776), edited by R[oy] H. Campbell, A[ndrew] S. Skinner, and W[illiam] B. Todd, 2 vols. (Oxford: Clarendon Press, 1976)

Smith, Billy G. '"The Best Poor Man's Country": Living Standards of the "Lower Sort" in Late Eighteenth-Century Philadelphia,' *Working Papers from the Regional Economic History Research Center*, II (No. 4, 1979), 1–70

—— *The 'Lower Sort': Philadelphia's Laboring People, 1750–1800* (Ithaca, New York: Cornell University Press, [1990])

The Social Sciences in Historical Study: A Report of the Committee on Historiography, [edited by Hugh G. J. Aitken], Social Science Research Council, Bulletin 64 (New York: Social Science Research Council, 1965)

[South Carolina. Commissioners for Ascertaining the Progressive Depreciation of the Paper Currency]. *An Accurate Table, Ascertaining the Progressive Depreciation of the Paper-Currency, in the Province of South-Carolina during the Late Usurpation ...* (Charleston, South Carolina: John Wells, 1781)

Stabilization of the Domestic and International Economy, edited by Karl Brunner and Allan H. Meltzer, Carnegie-Rochester Conference Series on Public Policy, Vol. 5 (Amsterdam: North-Holland Publishing Company, 1977)

Studies in Economics and Industrial Relations, by Wesley C. Mitchell *et al.*

(Philadelphia, Pennsylvania: University of Pennsylvania Press, 1941)

A Table Shewing the Value of Old Tenor Bills, in Lawful Money ([Boston, Massachusetts: Samuel Kneeland and Timothy Green(?), 1750])

Taylor, George Rogers. 'Wholesale Commodity Prices at Charleston, South Carolina, 1732–1791,' *Journal of Economic and Business History*, iv (February 1932), 356–77

—— 'Wholesale Commodity Prices at Charleston, South Carolina, 1796–1861,' *Journal of Economic and Business History*, iv (August 1932), 848–[76]

Trends in the American Economy in the Nineteenth Century, edited by William N. Parker, National Bureau of Economic Research, Studies in Income and Wealth. Vol. 24 (Princeton, New Jersey: Princeton University Press, 1960)

Turvey, Ralph. *Consumer Price Indexes: An ILO Manual* (Geneva, Switzerland: International Labour Office, 1989)

Ulmer, Melville J. *The Economic Theory of Cost of Living Index Numbers* (New York: Columbia University Press, 1949)

[United States. Congress]. *American State Papers: Documents, Legislative and Executive, of the Congress of the United States*, 38 vols. (Washington, D.C.: Gales and Seaton, 1832–61)

[United States. Congress. Joint Economic Committee]. *Study of Employment, Growth, and Price Levels: Hearings before the Joint Economic Committee, Congress of the United States . . . April 7, 8, 9, and 10, 1959*, 86th Congress, 2d Session, 10 parts in 13 vols. (Washington, D.C.: United States Government Printing Office, 1959–60)

[United States. Congress. Senate. Committee on Finance]. *Wholesale Prices, Wages, and Transportation: Report by Mr. [Nelson W.] Aldrich, from the Committee on Finance, March 3, 1893*, 52nd Congress, 2d Session, Senate Report No. 1394 [Serial Set No. 3074], 4 parts (Washington, D.C.: United States Government Printing Office, 1893)

[United States. Department of Commerce. Bureau of the Census]. *Historical Statistics of the United States, Colonial Times to 1970*, [3d ed.], 2 vols. (Washington, D.C.: United States Government Printing Office, 1975)

—— *Statistical Abstract of the United States*, 109th ed. (Washington, D.C.: United States Government Printing Office, 1989)

[United States. Department of Labor. Bureau of Labor Statistics]. *BLS Handbook of Methods*, Bureau of Labor Statistics, Bulletin 2285 (Washington, D.C.: United States Government Printing Office, 1988)

—— *The Consumer Price Index: Concepts and Content over the Years*, Bureau of Labor Statistics, Report 517, rev. ed. (Washington, D.C.: United States Government Printing Office, 1978)

—— *Index Numbers of Wholesale Prices in the United States and Foreign Countries*, Bureau of Labor Statistics, Bulletin No. 284 (Washington, D.C.: United States Government Printing Office, 1921)

[United States. President]. *Economic Report of the President* (Washington, D.C.: United States Government Printing Office, 1991)

Vigneti, P. V. N. *Changes faits sur le cours de papier-monnoies, depuis leur origine, 31 août 1789, jusqu'au 30 ventôse de l'an IV . . . auquel on a joint un tableau progressif de dépréciation vraie . . .* (Paris: Gueffier and the Author, 1797)

Walsh, Lorena S. 'Plantation Management in the Chesapeake, 1620–1820,' *Journal of Economic History*, XLIX (June 1989), 393–406

Warner, Sam Bass, Jr. *Writing Local History: The Use of Social Statistics*, Technical Leaflet 7, rev. ed. (Nashville, Tennessee: American Association for State and Local History, 1970)

Warren, G[eorge] F., F[rank] A. Pearson, and Herman M. Stoker. *Wholesale Prices for 213 Years, 1720 to 1932*, Cornell University, Agricultural Experiment Station, Memoir 412 (Ithaca, New York: The University, 1932)

Webster, Pelatiah. *Political Essays on the Nature and Operation of Money, Public Finances, and Other Subjects: Published during the American War, and Continued to the Present Year, 1791* (Philadelphia, Pennsylvania: Joseph Crukshank, 1791)

Wesley Clair Mitchell: The Economic Scientist, edited by Arthur F. Burns (New York: National Bureau of Economic Research, 1952)

Wetzel, William A. *Benjamin Franklin as an Economist*, Johns Hopkins University Studies in Historical and Political Science, 13th Ser., No. 9 (Baltimore, Maryland: Johns Hopkins Press, 1895)

Woodward, Donald [M.] 'Wage Rates and Living Standards in Pre-Industrial England,' *Past & Present: A Journal of Historical Studies*, XCI (May 1981), 28–46

Wrigley, E[dward] A., and R. S. Schofield. *The Population History of England, 1641–1871: A Reconstruction* (Cambridge, Massachusetts: Harvard University Press, 1981)

Zarnowitz, Victor, and Geoffrey H. Moore. 'Major Changes in Cyclical Behavior,' in *The American Business Cycle: Continuity and Change*, edited by Robert J. Gordon, National Bureau of Economic Research, *Studies in Business Cycles*, Vol. 25 (Chicago: University of Chicago Press, 1986), pp. 519–82

GAYLORD S